I0756456

Basque Politics Series
No. 12

Macbeth in Basque

William Shakespeare

Translated by Bingen Ametzaga

With an introduction by
Xabier Irujo

Center for Basque Studies
University of Nevada, Reno

This book was published with generous financial assistance from the Basque Government

Basque Politics Series, No. 12
Series Editor: Xabier Irujo
Center for Basque Studies
University of Nevada, Reno
Reno, Nevada 89557
http://basque.unr.edu

Introduction translated by Jennifer Ottman
Preface translated by Cameron J. Watson

Book design: Juan San Martin

Library of Congress Cataloging-in-Publication Data

Names: Shakespeare, William, 1564-1616, author. | Ametzaga, Bingen, 1901-1969, translator. | Irujo Ametzaga, Xabier, writer of introduction. | Shakespeare, William, 1564-1616. Macbeth. | Shakespeare, William, 1564-1616. Macbeth. Basque.
Title: Macbeth in Basque / William Shakespeare ; translated by Bingen Ametzaga ; with an introduction by Xabier Irujo.
Other titles: Macbeth
Description: University of Nevada, Reno : Center for Basque Studies, 2017. | Series: Basque politics series ; No. 12 | A bilingual edition with parallel text in English and Basque. | Includes bibliographical references and index.
Identifiers: LCCN 2016047962 | ISBN 9781935709725 (pbk. : alk. paper)
Subjects: LCSH: Macbeth, King of Scotland, active 11th century--Drama. | Regicides--Drama. | Scotland--Drama. | GSAFD: Tragedies.
Classification: LCC PR2795.B32 M332 2017 | DDC 822.3/3--dc23 LC record available at https://na01.safelinks.protection.outlook.com/?url=https%3A%2F%2Flccn.loc.gov%2F2016047962&data=01%7C01%7Cdmontero%40unr.edu%7Ccf90223a134c4612b65508d46fa7b592%7C523b4bfc0ebd4c03b2b96f6a17fd31d8%7C1&sdata=UVLiH2HmO132YK%2Fx6KjPxZ9IpYsqoiuREwhBPd801Ss%3D&reserved=0

Contents

Introduction

The *Río de la Plata* had set sail from Havana on March 12, 1942. A few days later, off the northern coast of Brazil, it came to a halt. Bingen Ametzaga left the manuscript on which he was working on the small desk in his cabin and, following the captain's orders, put on his lifejacket and headed to the main deck.

On December 7, 1941, the Japanese had bombed Pearl Harbor, leading to a rupture in diplomatic relations between Japan and the United States and the entry of the United States into World War II. In virtue of the Tripartite Pact signed between Germany, Italy, and Japan on September 27, 1940, Nazi Germany declared war on the United States on December 11.

Admiral Karl Dönitz, commander of the German Navy's submarine fleet, immediately launched Operation Drumbeat (*Unternehmen Paukenschlag*), which consisted in sending out five type IX submarines with orders to sink all cargo ships they encountered. In the first month and a half of 1942, Dönitz's wolf pack (*Wolfsrudel*) succeeded in sinking twenty-two merchant ships.

This operation targeting the U.S. East Coast was so successful that a successor, Operation New Land (*Operation Neuland*), was immediately launched against merchant shipping in Caribbean waters. The objective in this case was to interrupt the supplies of oil and aluminum transported to the United States and the United Kingdom from Caribbean ports. Between February 16 and March 23, 1942, eleven German submarines sank forty-six ships and damaged another ten.

One of these submarines, active off the coast of the Guianas, had surfaced and ordered the commander of the *Río de la Plata* to halt the ship on the open sea. The crew, the majority of whom were Basques, Spaniards, and Jews fleeing occupied Europe, were tense with anxiety. A small group of armed men came on board and requisitioned food, other essentials, and—it was rumored—some money and other valuables. After several hours during which the ship remained unmoving on the open sea, observing the submarine where it had halted some distance away, threatening the Argentine ship with its torpedoes, the armed men left the ship. The submarine turned around and allowed the *Río de la Plata* to continue its voyage without further incident.

It was not a coincidence that the submarine was in those waters, nor that it allowed the Argentine-flagged ship to continue on its way. Only two months earlier, between January 15 and 18, 1942, the Third Pan-American Congress had taken place in Rio de Janeiro. At that conference, at which six South American countries had declared war on the Axis nations, and others had suspended diplomatic relations with them, Argentina and Chile decided to maintain their relations with Nazi Germany and its allies.

After interminable hours of apprehension, the passengers returned to their cabins. Bingen took off his lifejacket and continued working on his manuscript. He was finishing the first translation into Euskara of one of Shakespeare's classic plays, *Macbeth.*

The Spy Who Translated Shakespeare

Bingen Ametzaga was born in Algorta, a village in the municipality of Getxo, Bizkaia, on July 4, 1901, in his family's ancestral house, known as Iturrieta and located on Avenida Basagoiti. He began to write at a very young age, and he was seventeen when he published his first works in various journals in the Basque Country. Together with his friend José Olivares, a writer, he founded the journal *El Gobela* (The Gobela River), which his brother Ramón edited and managed. Considered one of the poets of the "Aitzol Generation" by the Guatemalan journal *Euzko Gogoa,* he wrote extensively in both Spanish and Euskara prior to the outbreak of the Spanish Civil War in 1936, although the majority of his poetry from this period has unfortunately been lost. He submitted a number of poems in Euskara to the competitions organized by Fr. José de Ariztimuño between 1933 and 1934 and won several prizes.

After graduating with degrees in law and commercial engineering, he became deeply knowledgeable in the years between 1920 and 1936 in the subjects around which his intellectual life would revolve from the outbreak of war in 1936 until his death. In 1921, at the age of twenty, he spoke and wrote Euskara, Spanish, English, and French. Between this date and 1936, he perfected his knowledge of Latin, Classical Greek, Italian, and German, all languages from which he would translate numerous works, especially poetry, into Euskara. During these years, his only period of relative spiritual tranquility and material comfort, Bingen acquired comprehensive familiarity with Basque history and culture, on which over the course of his life he would give more than five hundred lectures,[1] publish more than five hundred newspaper articles[2] and around fifty translations, and write ten books, five of which have been published.[3] In 1933, he began to combine his law practice with teaching, offering classes in history and literature at a secondary school, the Instituto de Segunda Enseñanza, in Getxo, where he was also named a justice of the peace.

---

1 Some of his lectures were collected in his book *El hombre vasco* (The Basque man) (Buenos Aires: Ekin, 1963).

2 An anthology of Bingen Ametzaga's newspaper articles has been published in the two volumes of *Nostalgia* (Donostia: Ed. J. A. Ascunce, 1993), prepared by his daughter Arantzazu Ametzaga, who also wrote a prologue to the collection.

3 Three of his works, carefully compiled and organized by his wife, Mercedes Iribarren, were published in Bingen Ametzaga, *Obras completas* (Complete works), 3 vols. (Bilbao: La Gran Enciclopedia Vasca, 1979). These three volumes (intended to be the first three of twelve) include three of his previously published works, *El hombre vasco*, *Hombres de la Compañía Guipuzcoana* (Men of the Compañía Guipuzcoana), and *El elemento vasco en el siglo XVIII venezolano* (The Basque element in the Venezuelan eighteenth century). Also published, in addition to these titles, were *Jesús Muñoz Tebar*, with E. Pardo Stolk (Caracas: Fundación Eugenio Mendoza, 1959) and *Vicente Antonio de Icuza, comandante de corsarios* (Vicente Antonio de Icuza, commander of corsairs) (Caracas: Ediciones del Cuatricentenario de Caracas, 1966). These historical works are complemented by a dictionary of idioms and by Ametzaga's poetry. Santiago Onaindia's *Milla Euskal-Olerki Eder* (1954) includes a small sample of Ametzaga's Euskara poetry, one of the few surviving vestiges of his pre-1937 poetry.

Following General Franco's military uprising and the consequent outbreak of war in July 1936, on November 12 of the same year, Ametzaga was appointed the Basque government's general director of primary education by Jesús Mª Leizaola, the minister of justice and culture. As Leizaola wrote, Ametzaga held this position "precisely on account of his demonstrated interest in the cultivation of Euskara. I have to explain how different the essential concern that he had to address in occupying this position was; at that time, its importance was even greater than that of purely cultural matters, and it was common to both of us, at the absolute forefront of attention in those days. . . . In the weeks preceding the appointment, German planes had bombed Bilbao and Las Arenas in support of Franco's rebellion; ninety-six people, including eighteen women and children, died in indiscriminate air raids such as those mentioned. In his position as general director of primary education, Ametzaga had one primordial concern, as I did: keeping the schools and school-age children from being hit by enemy bombs. I can affirm that [Ametzaga] scoured all of Vizcaya in search of possible places of refuge for the children and their instructors, just as he also promoted and selected locations where the mayors felt this primary and fundamental concern. None of his choices were mistaken, and even if there were, of course, children who were victims of the air raids, they were never at school or in school groups. . . . When I appointed him, without him having sought the position at all, he made his appearance in my office in a way that was surprising for its extreme discretion. It was not shyness; his nearsightedness gave him a particular manner characteristic of the uncertainty or prudence with which people who have difficulties with their vision move. What I knew about him, besides his love for and cultivation of the Basque language, especially in poetry, was that he was a lawyer and a municipal judge in Getxo."[4]

With the war raging and the front line driven back to no more than thirty miles from Bilbao, on December 4, 1936, he issued the order for the creation of the first Basque school or *ikastola* under the terms of the 1936 Statute of Autonomy (*Estatuto de Autonomía*).[5] Alongside the foundation of the *ikastolas,* Bingen

4 Typed letter from Jesús Mª de Leizaola to Arantzazu Ametzaga, including the first draft of an introduction to Bingen Ametzaga's complete works, Paris, February 15, 1979.

5 *Diario oficial del País Vasco,* no. 59/36 (December 1936): 469.

undertook the task of translating textbooks into Euskara and creating the first teacher-training schools. In order to keep the children away from the bombs of the German, Italian, and Spanish planes, the *ikastolas* were initially created in small towns without military or strategic interest, far from the front lines. Nevertheless, starting in April 1937, the air forces began a campaign of terror bombings in which the targets were precisely these locations, towns such as Gernika, which was entirely destroyed on April 26, 1937, causing more than two thousand deaths, primarily among the civilian population.

In view of the more than one thousand bombing operations recorded in the Basque Country between July 22, 1936, and August 1937, and faced with the imminent fall of Bilbao, Ametzaga had to dedicate himself starting in late April 1937 to the task of dismantling these *ikastolas* and arranging the children's evacuation abroad. Many of the thirty-two thousand Basque children evacuated on English and French ships between April and August of that year had lost all contact with their families, or else their relatives were persecuted and had gone into exile or were in prison. The evacuation of these children demanded the opening of sea routes, primarily to the United Kingdom, France, Belgium, Mexico, and the USSR, and the simultaneous organization in those countries of school colonies where the children could be housed and continue their studies.[6]

After Bilbao was taken by General Franco's troops and their allies, the regime sentenced Ametzaga to death and ordered the seizure of all his property, on the grounds that he was "one of those who caused the ruin of Vizcaya." Five days before going into exile, at three in the morning on June 14, 1937, to be precise, with only the sacristan and a young altar boy as witnesses, he married Mercedes Iribarren, the younger daughter of the industrialist Inocencio Iribarren, in the parish church of Areeta, partially damaged by German aerial bombardment.

The victory of Franco's troops would likewise put an end to all the Basque government's efforts, and the Plentzia *ikastola,* like all the rest, would be closed. The Basque language would be prohibited, and its use at home and in public, both written and spoken, would be persecuted.

---

6 Arantxa Beti, "El exilio vasco: Educación-universidad," in José A. Ascunce, *La cultura del exilio vasco* (Donostia, 1994), 2: 211.

A few days before the fall of Bilbao, the Basque government had put Ametzaga in charge of the colony of five hundred Basque refugee children in Donibane Garazi, Lower Navarre, which meant that he had to set out for the port of Santander that very night. At the time, the last shells were falling on Bilbao prior to the fascist troops' entry into the city. His daughter, Arantzazu Ametzaga, has recounted the story of how Ametzaga urged Leizaola to abandon the Basque government's headquarters in Bilbao's Hotel Carlton as shells were exploding around them, while Leizaola showed not the slightest sign of agitation. Finally leaving Bilbao behind and crossing the area occupied by Italian troops between the capital and Getxo, Ametzaga said goodbye there to his mother, whom he would never see again. María Aresti, seventy-five years old, was thus left widowed and alone in Iturrieta, the house where she was born. Years later, her son would learn that María Aresti was sentenced to drink castor oil, had her head shaved, and was forced to abandon her house and property on the orders of the Central Administrative Commission for Seized Property (*Comisión Central Administradora de Bienes Incautados*),[7] for the crime of being the mother of three exiles. Despite everything, a friendly family in Getxo took her in and gave her the opportunity to rebuild her life.

The evacuation of these five hundred children by bus from Bilbao to Santander was an odyssey. Throughout the night, Heinkel He51 fighter planes and the new Messerschmitt Bf 109s unceasingly strafed the endless convoys of civilians heading into exile. After several anxious days, they were able to embark on the *Ploubazlanec,* with the mentioned colony at Donibane Garazi as their destination. Setting up, organizing, and supervising these colonies of Basque children was Ametzaga's primary concern during his first three years in exile. In general terms, it was a

7 In virtue of an order issued by the Getxo municipal administration on November 26, 1938, in accordance with the finding of culpability made by the general in command of the Military Division on April 23 of the same year, María Aresti was fined 100,000 pesetas, to be paid within two weeks, in order to release the embargo that affected all her property, all this under the terms of the decree law of January 10, 1937. In this way, María was able to buy back Iturrieta, but she had to sell it not long afterward, her resources having been exhausted by the loans she had taken out in order to pay the fines. The sale of Iturrieta, the house where he was born, was a harsh blow for Bingen, by that time in exile in Uruguay. It was a first omen, a sure sign that he would not recover his old life and that his return would be postponed.

matter of organizing *ikastolas* in exile, and they were structured accordingly. In addition to the children's safety and health, one of the fundamental objectives of the colonies, as of the ephemeral *ikastolas* of 1936-37, "was to preserve and spread the use of Euskara, which was not only taught as another course or used as a means of expression for the study of other subjects; rather, its use was intended to be the most characteristic and defining sign of a people who had seen themselves forced to leave their territory on account of the war. For this reason, the teachers were concerned to promote the use of Euskara in the children's daily life."[8]

Living in Paris, Ametzaga devoted his efforts between 1937 and June 1940 to consolidating the colonies and supervising their operation in the United Kingdom. This task required him to make periodic visits to Great Britain, where there were various colonies of exiled children, including those of Liverpool, Cardiff, and the Isle of Wight, which were of considerable size. From August to September 1938, he worked in collaboration with the central office of the Spanish Republic's embassy in London to organize the provision of clothing, medicine, and other essentials for the children, as well as Euskara classes and the minimum materials needed to hold them. He was also assigned the task of organizing a library for the Basque delegation during his two years of residence in Paris.

The day that Germany invaded Poland, giving rise to World War II, Ametzaga's second daughter, Begoña, was born in Paris. Fearing the use of gas, as in the Great War, mother and daughter each had to carry a gas mask. After a tense winter, during which it had begun to be said that the best way out for the Basques was to sail to the Americas, Germany's spring blitzkrieg against France surprised Ametzaga in Paris, a city he left on the same day that the first armored units entered it, June 14, 1940. When the family arrived by train in Bordeaux, the Germans had already occupied that city.

With German troops occupying the northern Basque Country, Ametzaga, who was wanted by the Gestapo, was taken to the headquarters of the occupying forces. Nevertheless, to his surprise, he was not detained, and he suffered no consequences from the interrogation, very possibly because the occupying forces

8 Arantxa Beti, "El exilio vasco: Educación-universidad," in José A. Ascunce, *La cultura del exilio vasco* (Donostia, 1994), 2: 212.

lacked the necessary information and the personnel to proceed to detentions at that time. In any case, uncertain about their fate in occupied Europe and unsure where to flee or by what route, Ametzaga and his wife decided to leave their two daughters in the care of Mercedes's sister and travel to Marseilles, where they ultimately embarked on the *Alsina* along with a sizeable group of Basques, supporters of the Spanish Republic, and Jews, setting sail for the Americas on January 15, 1941.

When they left on the *Alsina,* they did not know for certain what country would be their destination. They would not see their daughter Mirentxu again until she was nine years old, and Ametzaga would not see his daughter Begoña again until a few days before his death.

After a voyage lasting a year and three months, marked by great suffering and uncertainty (detention in a Vichy French concentration camp in North Africa, along with a group of Jews; the interception of the ship carrying them to Argentina by a German submarine in the Caribbean), husband and wife reached Buenos Aires on April 15, 1942.

The Western Hemisphere offered Ametzaga the opportunity to take up once more his intellectual work of popularizing Basque language and culture, which had been interrupted by events between 1936 and 1942. During this period, he wrote the first of his six poetic works, *Guerra y destierro* (War and exile).[9] The unpublished book consisted of a total of fifty poems, twenty-six of which have disappeared. As the poet Rafael Alberti would also do, Ametzaga narrated the itinerary of the exodus from Marseilles to Buenos Aires, in a tone that was sometimes hopeful and more often nostalgic.

The years 1942 and 1943 were ones of tireless activity. It

9 He would go on to write four additional volumes of poetry, although they have unfortunately survived only in very fragmentary form: *Ángelus* (Angelus) (1942-44), *Rincones mágicos* (Magic corners) (1942-44), *Últimos poemas* (Last poems) (1945-58), and a small jewel of the Basque poetry and dialectology of the exile community, *Errimiña* (1943-68). He also left behind a small work of prose poetry about his native Getxo, titled *Charlas de Axerrota* (Axerrota conversations) (1943), a chapter of which, "Sinfonía de Getxo" (Getxo symphony), was published in Arantzazu Ametzaga, *Nostalgia*, 2: 316-18. During the author's lifetime, the same chapter was published in the Mexican journal *Euzko Deya* in 1946 and, years later, in the Caracas journal *Euzko Gaztedi* in 1957. Another chapter, "Intermedio sentimental" (Sentimental interlude), was also published in the Buenos Aires journal *Euzko Deya* on June 6, 1943.

would seem that his prolonged inactivity at sea had unleashed in Ametzaga an almost titanic desire to live, to battle to rebuild his life and the life of Basque culture in exile. A week after reaching shore in Buenos Aires, he was working as a bookkeeper in a sandal factory, a job that would give him a certain degree of financial stability. Before he had been in the Argentine capital two months, he was immersed in the creation of the Basque Studies Institute of the Americas (*Instituto Americano de Estudios Vascos*), the plans for which he had heard about during the long voyage from Marseilles and of which he became a co-founder. During the months from May to December, he undertook what would become a lengthy series of lectures, later compiled in one of his most representative works, *El hombre vasco* (The Basque man), published in 1967.

The new year, 1943, opened with a blessing, the birth of his third daughter, Arantzazu, in January. At the beginning of the year, he had been called on to join the organizing committee for the Montevideo Basque Cultural Week, requiring him to move to that city. At the same time, he began in mid-1943 to organize a group of seven Basque secret agents in Uruguay who collaborated with the Allied war effort in contact with the Roosevelt administration's newly created Office of Strategic Services (OSS). The objective of this group of agents would be to locate and neutralize fascist and Nazi cells in the country. They were in contact with other cells of Basque agents based in various Western Hemisphere countries, primarily in Brazil, Argentina, and Chile. The two latter countries were reluctant to break off relations with Nazi Germany, and a sizeable network of Axis agents and their allies were active in them.

The message of these networks of Axis agents and sympathizers in the countries of South America was basically that the Axis countries and their satellites, such as Italy, Spain, and Austria, were Catholic, while the majority of the Allied countries were Protestant. It is consequently no surprise that both in the networks of Axis sympathizers and in those of Basque agents there were numerous priests, including Fr. Pedro Goikoetxea, who would work closely with Ametzaga and his team of agents in Uruguay.

Alongside these activities, Ametzaga took on the organization of Montevideo's Great Basque Cultural Week (*La Gran Semana Cultural Vasca*) in the fall of 1943, an event of immense significance in the life of the Basque exile community in the Americas. Aware that the war was dragging on and filled with uncertainty about the international politics of General Franco's government, the Basque community used the Cultural Week to introduce themselves to Uruguay and to the Western Hemisphere as a whole, as an integral part of the new continent's cultural, political, intellectual, and social life.

Popularly known as the "fifteen-day week" (October 30 to November 15, 1943), the Great Basque Week was the first public celebration organized by the Basque exile community with an emphatically international and political nature. For the first time, a folkloric and cultural festival of this size was held with the doors thrown open to the general public of the Americas, and for the first time, prominent figures in Western Hemisphere intellectual, artistic, and above all, political life were invited to participate. In addition to being a cultural event, the Basque Week was an act of defiance by the Allied democracies against the Axis dictatorships. It was a salute and a demonstration of profound gratitude to figures such as Roberto Ortiz, the president of the Argentine Republic, who was of Basque heritage; Juan José Amezaga, the president of the Eastern Republic of Uruguay, another Basque; and other prominent figures in the continent's political life who not only permitted, but favored, facilitated, and financed the adoption of this population driven from its homeland, defeated and humiliated at home.

However, 1943 would also lay the foundation for still other developments. Following a series of contacts made in connection with the Basque Week, Ametzaga and the rector of the humanities faculty of the Universidad de la República del Uruguay, Dr. Jiménez de Aretxaga, a professor of constitutional law, agreed to create a department of Basque studies, including a chair in Basque language, in the faculty of humanities and sciences. This was the first chair of its kind in the Americas and the first department of Basque studies outside the Basque Country.

Similarly, 1944 again opened with an entirely new cycle of activities. Motivated by the Normandy landings on June 6, 1944, and the liberation of the northern Basque Country, Ametzaga participated in various events of a political nature. On May 13, the Plaza Gernika was dedicated in Montevideo as a memorial to those killed in the bombing and as a recognition by the Uruguayan authorities of the Basque exile community and, by extension, all the victims of Axis atrocities. The ceremony was attended by the mayor of Montevideo, Juan Fabiani, along with other Uruguayan politicians and various representatives of the Belgian, Czechoslovak, Mexican, Polish, and Venezuelan diplomatic delegations, and it turned out to be a highly significant event in the country's political life. Likewise, following the liberation of France, an event was organized at the Club Uruguay to found an aid committee on behalf of the population of the three Basque territories occupied by the Germans between 1940 and their liberation in 1944.

At the Yalta Conference, held on February 11, 1945, the Allied leaders ratified the policy agreed at the Teheran Conference on December 1, 1943, regarding the reestablishment of democracy in the countries liberated from Nazi Germany's control and in the Axis's former European satellites. The Basque delegations were very active in relation to this issue. The president of the Basque government-in-exile, Jose A. Agirre, worked closely with the prime minister of the Spanish Republic, José Giral, as they advocated before the United Nations committee investigating the "Franco case," and the new international body sanctioned General Franco's government for its dictatorial nature and its connivance with the Axis powers during World War II. The resolution was reaffirmed by the General Assembly on December 12, 1946, and the Security Council condemned the Spanish government in the following terms:

> (a) In origin, nature, structure and general conduct, the Franco regime is a fascist regime patterned on, and established largely as a result of aid received from, Hitler's Nazi Germany and Mussolini's Fascist Italy.
> (b) During the long struggle of the United Nations against Hitler and Mussolini, Franco, despite continued Allied protests, gave very substantial aid to the enemy Powers. First, for example, from 1941 to 1945, the Blue Infantry Division, the Spanish Legion of Volunteers and the Salvador Air Squadron fought against Soviet Russia on the Eastern front. Second, in the summer of 1940, Spain seized Tangier in breach of international statute, and as a result of Spain maintaining a large army in Spanish Morocco large numbers of Allied troops were immobilized in North Africa.
> (c) Incontrovertible documentary evidence establishes that Franco was a guilty party with Hitler and Mussolini in

> the conspiracy to wage war against those countries which eventually in the course of the world war became banded together as the United Nations. It was part of the conspiracy that Franco's full belligerency should be postponed until a time to be mutually agreed upon.
>
> The General Assembly, Convinced that the Franco Fascist Government of Spain, which was imposed by force upon the Spanish people with the aid of the Axis Powers and which gave material assistance to the Axis Powers in the war, does not represent the Spanish people, and by its continued control of Spain is making impossible the participation of the Spanish people with the peoples of the United Nations in international affairs; Recommends that the Franco Government of Spain be debarred from membership in international agencies established by or brought into relationship with the United Nations, and from participation in conferences or other activities which may be arranged by the United Nations or by these agencies, until a new and acceptable government is formed in Spain.
>
> The General Assembly, Further, desiring to secure the participation of all peace-loving peoples, including the people of Spain, in the community of nations, Recommends that if, within a reasonable time, there is not established a government which derives its authority from the consent of the governed, committed to respect freedom of speech, religion and assembly and to the prompt holding of an election in which the Spanish people, free from force and intimidation and regardless of party, may express their will, the Security Council consider the adequate measures to be taken in order to remedy the situation; Recommends that all Members of the United Nations immediately recall from Madrid their Ambassadors and Ministers plenipotentiary accredited there. The General Assembly further recommends that the States Members of the Organization report to the Secretary-General and to the next session of the Assembly what action they have taken in accordance with this recommendation.[10]

It was a political victory for the Basque, Catalan, Galician, and Spanish democrats. Nevertheless, it was necessary to keep Franco out of the United Nations, thereby preventing the Spanish dicta-

---

10 United Nations General Assembly, Resolutions Adopted by the General Assembly during Its First Session, 39 (I), December 12, 1946, Relations of Members of the United Nations with Spain.

torship's integration into that body and forcing the dictator's fall.

During the years between 1944 and 1949, Ametzaga actively participated in the "Franco case" in Uruguay, seeking to stop the Uruguayan government from extending diplomatic recognition to the Spanish dictatorship. Of course, this was not a difficult task. Working closely with Dardo Regules, a senator from the Civic Action (*Acción Cívica*) party, who was also at that time the director of the daily newspaper *El Bien público*, Ametzaga met with Uruguay's president in 1945, Juan José Amezaga, and with his successors until 1954. From 1945 onward, the Uruguayan government's position with respect to General Franco's dictatorship was robust: the Republic of Uruguay would not recognize the Spanish military regime or accept its entrance into the United Nations. Along with Mexico, Uruguay was the only Western Hemisphere country that maintained unwavering support for the cause of the Catalan, Spanish, and Basque peoples in opposition to Franco's dictatorship throughout the ten years following the end of World War II. Session after session, at each United Nations General Debate between 1945 and 1955, Uruguay denounced the abuses committed by the dictatorial government against its own people.

After the war's end, Ametzaga and other OSS agents were invited to the U.S. embassy in Montevideo, where a ceremony was held to recognize all these men and women who helped the Allied effort. Ametzaga attended together with his daughter Arantzazu. As part of the program that day, the documentary *Nazi Concentration Camps* was shown, a film first exhibited during the Nuremberg trials as evidence of the Nazi horror. Arantzazu has said that she saw her father cry, because even as someone who had been interned in a concentration camp and had dedicated several years of his life to fighting Axis agents, he had not believed what some of the Jews who escaped to the Americas with him had told him about the gas chambers and other atrocities. He discovered that he had been unable to grasp the real dimensions of the Holocaust until that moment.

At the age of forty-nine, Ametzaga's life was marked by suffering, upheaval, and serious illness. The Spanish state's gradual entrance into the United Nations and its international recognition starting in 1951 under the cover of the Cold War, his mother's death years before, the definitive prolongation of his exile, his constant financial struggles, and severe overwork culminated in a nervous breakdown that left him sunk in a deep depression. He gave up everything, except the chair of Basque language in the department of Basque studies at the Universidad de la República, for a period of ten months.

On the occasion of UNESCO's Eighth General Conference in Montevideo, Justino Zabala, the conference's president for its Montevideo session and Uruguay's minister of public education and social security, appointed Ametzaga the ministry's delegate to UNESCO. His task was the overall coordination of the organization of the session, to be held in Montevideo during the month of December. For that purpose, he worked closely with Antonio Gamarra, the head of UNESCO's press secretariat for South America. In collaboration with the rector of the Universidad de Montevideo, Ametzaga organized various lectures at the university for the UNESCO delegations, including a lecture given on December 6 of that year by the canon Alberto Onaindia, a Basque political exile with a doctorate in philosophy and theology from the Gregorian University in Rome, on the ties between the university and the people.

The subject of the Spanish government's admission to UNESCO—a preliminary step toward its admission to the United Nations—remained a live issue in a democracy like that of Uruguay. During the thirty days of the General Conference, Ametzaga wrote at least fifteen newspaper articles. Zabala allowed Ametzaga to raise the Basque problem in the assembly itself and seated the Basque government's representatives in the assembly. In the presence of the Spanish dictatorship's delegate, who was attending a UNESCO assembly for the first time, Zabala himself read out the endless lists of teachers who had been fired, exiled, and shot by General Franco's government and its measures regarding education in Spain (obligation to learn the dictatorship's political principles, prohibition of the use of indigenous languages, censorship . . .). It was an authentic lesson in democracy that the evening daily *El Plata* welcomed with rejoicing; on November 6, 1954, the newspaper itself published the Spanish embassy's furious response to Minister Zabala's declarations concerning Uruguay's position with regard to Franco's government on the occasion of UNESCO's Eighth General Conference: "We do not dispute his right to think what he pleases—however poor his taste—in regard to a problem like that of Spain, which has already been judged by the unanimous consensus of the reasonable nations of the West, but we deny his right to make declarations as a minister of state. . . . It seems," from the Spanish ambassador's perspective, "absurd and inappropriate that the minister of public education should have had the bad taste to recall the unfriendly gesture made in Paris in 1952, when as a consequence of and by virtue of his anti-Spanish passion, Uruguay voted almost alone against Spain's admission to UNESCO." Zabala's reply was cutting: "It has been on account of my love for what is Spanish and what is Basque that I have done what I have done."

Having completed his translations of *Macbeth*, *Julius Caesar*, and *A Midsummer Night's Dream*, Ametzaga began his translation of *Hamlet* in late 1950, and in mid-1951, he sent the original to Andrés Irujo, who would publish it with the Buenos Aires publishing house Ekin in late 1952. This would be the only one of Ametzaga's four completed translations of Shakespeare's works that would be published during his lifetime. In 1951, Ametzaga began his translation of *Platero y yo* (Platero and I), a novel by the Spanish poet and winner of the 1956 Nobel prize in literature Juan Ramón Jiménez, which would be published under the title *Platero ta biok* in Montevideo in 1953.

Shakespeare in Time of War

Franco's dictatorship imposed a centralized and unitary state model in which there was no room for the national differences of Basques, Catalans, and Galicians. Consequently, use of and publication in the Basque and Catalan languages were prohibited in practically all aspects of public life, and the attempt was made to limit the use of these languages in the private sphere. With this aim, a monolingual Spanish administration, a similarly monolingual judicial system, and a Spanish-language educational system were imposed. In 1936, "prohibited" books, including all those written in Basque, were burned in public bonfires or removed from circulation in the public library system and educational institutions. Subsequently, the regime's official censorship was used to set up all kinds of administrative obstacles to the publication of books, periodicals, and all other printed media in Basque.

Confronted with this situation, Ametzaga's work dealt in depth with the issue of Euskara from a wide variety of angles, including political, administrative, linguistic, normative, historical-cultural, and popularizing perspectives.

During the years immediately following the conclusion of the Second Carlist War (1872-76), Euskara began to experience an accelerated process of social deracination. The loss of the war, the definitive centralization of education, and the parallel official establishment of Spanish as the sole language of instruction, in addition to new policies for the territory's administration and organization as part of the Spanish state, resulted in the culmination of a long process that entailed, among many other socio-cultural aspects, the relegation of the Basque language to the most limited family or rural circles and its consequent devaluation. Primo de Rivera's dictatorship (1923-31) only intensified Euskara's decline, the fruit of a lengthy tradition of linguistic policy.

This was the social and political situation that the generation of politicians who were part of the Basque community of political exiles had to face, before and after the 1936 war. The task of recovering Euskara had to begin with a socio-cultural policy of dignifying all things Basque in general and the Basque language in particular, as an element and vehicle of culture. This effort required a massive labor of popularization in all areas of Basque culture: history and language, law, folklore, art, economics . . . This is the context within which we should understand Ametzaga, a prolific popularizer of Basque language and culture, first in the Basque Country and subsequently in the Americas.

The fundamental requirement for the recovery of Euskara, above and beyond all other aspects that might be taken into account, was the urgent officialization and normalization of the language. Within the wide range of activity covered by the officialization of Euskara—Euskara in public administration, in the judicial system, in the country's cultural life, in the recovery of place names—Ametzaga stood out for his work in the area of education. As a politician and administrator, first in his position as general director of primary education (1936-37) and later in exile in Uruguay, Ametzaga at all times considered his primary political objective to be the creation of *ikastolas* and university centers where Basque language classes were taught. For this reason, he affirmed in 1956 that "the true Basque resurgence will have to be rooted in the primary schools: this and nothing else is the origin and foundation of the Euskara renaissance."[11]

11 "Pro resurgimiento del Euskera," lecture at the Basque Center of Caracas,

Ametzaga labored to create *ikastolas* in the midst of war (1936-37), *ikastolas* that adopted the form of colonies for refugee children in the first years of exile (1937-39), and *ikastolas* in the department of Basque Studies of the Universidad de la República del Uruguay and at Montevideo's Euskal Erria Basque center (1943-54).

Teaching in Euskara required a great deal of written material, such as textbooks, handbooks, dictionaries, and encyclopedias, both in order to train professional educators and for the students themselves. "We do not have a university, it's true," Ametzaga commented in this regard while in exile, "but it's no less true that, as Carlyle said, the true university today is books, and this is something that we can do. 'What books?' we will be asked. We could answer with the most worthy Father [Raimundo] Olabide that we need a flood of books, books of all kinds."[12]

Methods for learning Euskara constituted a bibliographical cluster of singular importance. With regard to books for learning Euskara, Ametzaga considered that, "fortunately, the times have passed in which methods of learning Euskara were learned exhibitions of the difficulties of our language. We have now come to understand the deep truth contained within that apparent paradox of Prevost when he advises us not to study a language's grammar until we already know the language."[13]

An important group of works to be published were what Ametzaga called "writers' tools," such as dictionaries and other bibliographical support materials. In his view, the Basque language lacked these materials in 1936: "It seems impossible that we still continue without a basic dictionary. Nevertheless, one that would be extremely useful, without supposing it to be definitive, could be prepared in a few months, based on Azkue's Basque-Spanish-French dictionary[14] and completed with

Caracas, January 13, 1956.

12 "Pro resurgimiento del Euskera," lecture at the Basque Center of Caracas, Caracas, January 13, 1956. Ametzaga also mentions, in addition to books, the importance of publishing periodicals for children and adults and of promoting the publication of a daily newspaper entirely in Euskara.

13 "Pro resurgimiento del Euskera," lecture at the Basque Center of Caracas, Caracas, January 13, 1956. Ametzaga also discusses this idea in detail in an article, "Grandeza y miseria de la gramática," Uruguay, 1953.

14 With regard to the dictionary compiled by Resurrección M. Azkue, a Basque grammarian and lover of Basque culture, Ametzaga commented, "The Basque translator must be provided, as soon as possible, with a complete dictionary of

thousands of common words taken from the people's ordinary speech, plus the hundreds or perhaps thousands of neologisms that, because they have already been adopted by Basque speakers or because of their indisputable clarity, can be considered worthy of definitive incorporation into our lexicon."[15] In addition to this general dictionary of the language, Ametzaga considered it urgent to publish a set of three supporting dictionaries, one each of rhymes, synonyms, and idioms; he himself had completed the third, "containing several thousand idioms," but still unpublished.[16] On repeated occasions, speaking in his role as a translator, Ametzaga lamented this lack of dictionaries. In effect, Ametzaga carried out his translation of Shakespeare's works without a good English-Euskara dictionary: "The first deficiency that the Basque translator has to lament is the lack of that dictionary for which we have clamored for decades. Every time I think that I set out to translate *Hamlet* with no dictionary but Bera-López Mendizabal's—it was only when I was almost done that I received Father Lhande's dictionary as a gift from a good friend, and it was after I had finished that my copy of Azkue's dictionary arrived—I can only wonder at my audacity . . . or my heedlessness."[17]

Original works written in Euskara were logically of special importance, since in Ametzaga's opinion, an abundant production of such works was the fundamental goal to which the Basque people should aspire, both in exile and in the context of the Basque Country's internal resistance to Franco's dictator-

---

his language, that dictionary for which the entry slips were already stored—at least many thousands of them—in the old teacher Azkue's old offices, so full of memories for me, there in the Calle Ribera, and the publication of which is the first duty of the Academy [Euzkaltzaindia, the Academy of the Basque Language]." "Traducción de obras literarias al euskera: Interés de estos trabajos y problemas que los mismos plantean," typescript, Montevideo, June 1954.

15 "Pro resurgimiento del Euskera," lecture at the Basque Center of Caracas, Caracas, January 13, 1956.

16 With regard to this aspect of his work, Ametzaga commented, "For my part, I have in recent years been modestly noting down every idiom or idiomatic phrase I have found in my reading of old and new authors. In this way, I have been able to come up with a small dictionary of a few thousand turns of phrase, to which I have frequently had recourse." In "Traducción de obras literarias al euskera: Interés de estos trabajos y problemas que los mismos plantean," Montevideo, June 1954.

17 "Traducción de obras literarias al euskera: Interés de estos trabajos y problemas que los mismos plantean," typescript, Montevideo, June 1954.

ship. Along the same lines, he pointed out the need to publish second or third editions of Basque classics. The promotion of creativity needed to be pursued by the institutions and cultural foundations of the Basques in exile (given that the publication of works in Basque was subject to persecution within the country), fostering publication through literary contests and the formation of groups that would work to increase the size of the reading public.

A final but no less important group of works that urgently needed to be published consisted, in Ametzaga's opinion, in translations of classics of world literature: "The progress made by philology in the last hundred years, the needs of the educated public, the spread of culture, the development of school organization have had the consequence that translation has become the paradigmatic employment of a humanistic education in our day."[18] In the context of policies to promote the spoken and written use of Basque, and in general of any minority language, translation had a threefold function, according to Ametzaga.

On the one hand, translation would give "our writers models worthy of imitation."[19] In Ametzaga's opinion, translation was the best way to read. In effect, translating a literary text imposes a twofold reading, syntactic and semantic. Translation thus offered an unmatched framework within which to address this difficult issue and definitively settle various primarily syntactic matters that remained to be determined in relation to literary Euskara. "The first thing that we have to do in addressing this fundamental topic," Ametzaga said, "is to become fully conscious, once and for all, of the fact that Euskara is a single language. The more it is studied, the more clearly this unity is seen. And the second is that, although the existence of various dialects and varieties is a fact, we must also keep in mind that this is every language's natural state; that as Breal, who has been so often mentioned, has said, 'A language's true life is concentrated in its dialects'; and that, in sum, we have arrived at the moment of finding good precisely in what is presented to us as an evil."[20]

18 "Traducción de obras literarias al euskera: Interés de estos trabajos y problemas que los mismos plantean," typescript, Montevideo, June 1954.

19 "Pro resurgimiento del Euskera," lecture at the Basque Center of Caracas, Caracas, January 13, 1956.

20 "Traducción de obras literarias al euskera: Interés de estos trabajos y problemas que los mismos plantean," typescript, Montevideo, June 1954.

Second, the translation of masterworks of world literature into Euskara meant a major step forward in the unification and normalization of the language, and therefore in the creation of literary Euskara. The Basque language was not yet normalized in 1936, and it would not be so in full until at least 1968, when a group of Basque specialists would gather to work on this delicate task. Nevertheless, the first efforts to normalize Basque and generate a common Basque language began to be made starting in the late nineteenth century. The lack of classic works in the vernacular, a literary history limited by the Basque people's own demographic reality, and many other socio-economic and cultural aspects that far exceed the scope of this brief essay contributed to the fact that Euskara's linguistic normalization remained pending at the beginning of the century. Starting in 1918, the Academy of the Basque Language (*Euskaltzaindia*) had to face more than a few difficulties with respect to the unification of the language, and these conflicts remained live issues in the first years of Basque political exile starting in 1936. Translation allowed the translator to use "a specified variety of the Basque language," with a view toward its subsequent unification. In this regard, as a disciple and friend of the great Basque grammarian Resurrección M. Azkue, Ametzaga felt that the dialect or linguistic variety that should serve as the basis for the generation of a normalized Basque language was what was known as the "unified Gipuzkoan dialect" (*Gipuzkera osotua*), which was the one spoken in the country's geographical heart and consequently the closest to all the others from a grammatical perspective. In effect, even though Ametzaga spoke in Bizkaian dialect, the one spoken in his native Algorta, he used the unified dialect in his Shakespeare translations.

Third, the translation of masterworks of world literature into Basque or other minority languages would also serve to attain objectives in the socio-linguistic sphere. The idea that there existed "languages of culture" and "of civilization" and other languages that were intrinsically, by their very nature, "unsuited" to express messages of world thought or scientific ideas was deeply rooted in Europe between the eighteenth and twentieth centuries. These conceptions had their origin in the Enlightenment. In June 1782, Johann Formey, the secretary of the Berlin Academy, announced a contest on the question "What facts have contributed to making French a language of universal character?" Antoine de Rivarol won the competition with a discourse titled *Sur l'universalité de la langue française* (On the universality of the French language), which was published in 1783. The author argued that French deserved the title of a universal language due to its "genius" or inner spirit, which endowed this language with greater clarity, rigor, expressive capacity, and rationality. In a word, French was the language of the Enlightenment, and French speakers were its vehicle; it was impossible to be an enlightened, sophisticated, and properly educated person without speaking French. This outlook was shared by a variety of authors of the time, who defended in different languages, with this or that set of criteria, the suitability of their own languages and their superiority over the rest.

Moreover, these prejudices would soon arrive in European legislative chambers and be written into law. On May 9, 1794, in revolutionary Paris, Henri Grégoire argued before the National Convention that, although under the monarchy the French language had scarcely generated a correct political vocabulary, nevertheless, the Revolution had made French the most appropriate language for expressing Jacobite ideals, since the remaining languages spoken in the republic were no more than "heavy and gross dialects without specific syntax, because language is always the measure of a people's genius."[21] The Convention unanimously approved a decree on the need to create a new French grammar and vocabulary and gave this new language the name of "French" and the title of *langue de la liberté* (language of liberty). In Grégoire's opinion, and in virtue of the laws passed by the Paris legislative assembly, the other languages spoken or written in the republic needed to be destroyed.

More than a century later, another author argued that languages are the reflection of a people's genius and that as a consequence, there were languages that could be considered "languages of culture," like Spanish and French, and others that simply could not be so considered, like Euskara: "It has long been my conviction that Basque, an interesting language to study, lacks the intrinsic conditions to serve as a means of ex-

---

21 Henri-Baptiste Grégoire, *Rapports de Henri Grégoire, ancien évêque de Blois, sur la bibliographie, la destruction des patois et les excès du vandalisme, faits à la convention du 22 germinal an 2 au 24 frimaire an III* (Caen and Paris: A. Massif/Delarocque, 1867), 17-18.

pression for a people who enter fully into modern spiritual life."[22] For the philosopher Miguel Unamuno, Spanish was the superior language, since "it is a more fully crafted, more integrated, more analytical language and lends itself more to the degree of culture we have attained."[23] Without specifying what a "language of culture" meant in this context, he set out as a rule that a language's status—classified as a language of culture or a rustic language—would always be the same, since an uncivilized language could not aspire to become a civilizing instrument.[24] The writer Pío Baroja added further considerations along these lines, affirming that "if some have wished to demonstrate that Basque is a language that can be transformed into a literary and scientific language, they have been a small number of cranks and a large number of Carlist Euskarans disguised as philologists, who believe that all the truth in the world is contained in Astete's catechism."[25]

In the opinion of these and other authors, there were "superior" and "inferior" peoples and languages, because it was "highly rational to suppose that the language of a people who are superior to another people in thought and culture will be, by the same token, superior to the language of that people."[26] The conclusion was therefore obvious: the imposition of French or Spanish in the schools and in all areas of the country's public life was not only a cultural necessity, but an imperative, such that the destruction of national languages, to the point of causing their disappearance, became a moral demand and a political necessity, ultimately a patriotic duty. Unamuno compared Euskara to an illness that had to be extirpated in good faith, for the good of the language's own speakers. On one occasion, he commented that he had received "a letter from Dr. Joaquín Costa lamenting the fact that Basque was disappearing, when it had so much interest for the study of Iberian antiquities. I had to reply, 'Very well, but I am not going to act to preserve what I believe is an illness in order to satisfy a pathologist.'"[27] Betrand de Barère had expressed

22 Miguel Unamuno, "La cuestión del vascuence," *Ensayos* (Salamanca, 1902), 374.

23 Miguel Unamuno, *Revista de Vizcaya*, Bilbao, February 15, 1886.

24 Miguel Unamuno, "Discurso de Unamuno a propósito de la oficialidad del castellano," *Diario de Sesiones del Congreso español*, September 18, 1931.

25 Pío Baroja, *El Imparcial,* August 31, 1901.

26 Miguel Unamuno, "La cuestión del vascuence," *Ensayos* (Salamanca, 1902), 382.

27 Miguel Unamuno, "Discurso de Unamuno a propósito de la oficialidad del

himself in the same terms from the tribune of the French National Convention on Tuesday, January 28, 1794, when he affirmed that "the language called Breton, the Basque language, and the German and Italian languages have perpetuated the reign of fanaticism and superstition, ensuring the domination of priests, nobles, and professional men, preventing the Revolution from penetrating nine important departments and perhaps aiding the enemies of France . . . Federalism and superstition speak Breton, emigration and hatred of the Republic speak German, counter-revolution speaks Italian, and fanaticism speaks Basque. Let us destroy these instruments of prejudice and error."[28]

It was precisely with the aim of confronting these prejudices that Ametzaga undertook the task of translating four of Shakespeare's major works. It was a message to the world: what Shakespeare composed in English could be expressed with an equal wealth of linguistic resources in Basque. In other words, there are no superior or inferior languages or cultures, there are simply different cultures, and this variety has to be cultivated, because it is precisely in this variety that the fundamental richness of human nature and the versatility of human thought are rooted.

Ametzaga's translation of Shakespeare's plays was therefore a response to three fundamental objectives:

1. Revitalizing the Basque language from the Americas. The basic aim of Ametzaga's work was to stimulate the publication of literary and scholarly works in exile, in order to subsequently introduce them into the Basque Country, given that, as we have previously had occasion to mention, the publication of Basque-language works inside the country was first prohibited for years, then persecuted and heavily censored during the later years of General Franco's regime.
2. Contributing to the normalization of Basque, an effort that would finally bear fruit in 1968. The immediate practical objective of Ametzaga's translations was basically to generate a linguistic model for a unified Basque language. The linguistic model Ametzaga defended in his translations was that of the Basque dialect of Gipuz-

castellano," *Diario de Sesiones del Congreso español*, September 18, 1931.

28 *Gazette nationale ou Le Moniteur universel*, 3d ser., vol. 6, no. 129 (nonidi, 9 pluviose, l'an 2e [Tuesday, January 28, 1794]), 5-8. See also *Recueil de lois et règlemens concernant l'instruction publique, depuis l'Edit de Henri IV en 1598 jusqu'à ce jour* (Paris: Brunot-Labbe, 1814), 1: 22-26.

koa and northern Navarre. In this regard, he followed the ideas of his teacher in this area, the eminent linguist Resurrección M. Azkue, and shared the views of Jokin Zaitegi, Nicolas Ormaetxea, and Andima Ibiñagabeitia. Years later, this model, first called "Unified Gipuzkoan" (*Gipuzkera osotua*) and today known as "Unified Euskara" (*Euskara batua*), would be the one finally institutionalized by the Academy of the Basque Language (*Euskaltzaindia*) in 1968.

3. Condemning the linguistic policy of the Spanish and French states. Editing and publishing Basque-language books in the Americas likewise served to demonstrate to the Spanish and French governments that while the authorities of both states persecuted or just tacitly denied the existence of Basque in the Basques' own land, the governments of states such as Uruguay, Argentina, Mexico, and Venezuela promoted its use and applauded the publication of works written in this language more than six thousand miles from Euskal Herria.

All these ideas were fermenting in Ametzaga's mind when he found himself on the *Río de la Plata* in 1942, facing that German submarine.

Shakespeare in Euskara

From the celebration of the Great Basque Week in Montevideo in 1943 onward, the Uruguayan people and their political representatives actively and decisively supported the Basque people's right to keep their language and culture alive both in the Basque Country itself and in the Americas. The president of the Republic of Uruguay in 1943 was Juan José Amezaga, the descendant of Basques from Algorta. Along with his wife, their daughters, and all his cabinet ministers, he participated directly in the events held during that fifteen-day cultural "week." His decided support for the Basque people's cause had great resonance in the country.

It was therefore not a coincidence that during the Southern Hemisphere fall of 1944, when speaking Euskara in the Basque Country was a crime, the first chair of the Basque language in the Americas was created at the Universidad de la República del Uruguay in Montevideo. The creation of the chair was due fundamentally to the interest, efforts, and generosity of individuals such as Adolfo Berro, a professor of phonetics and experimental philology and director of the philology faculty; Carlos Vaz-Ferreira, rector of the university between 1935 and 1941 and subsequently dean of the humanities faculty, within which the Euskara chair was located; Leopoldo Agorio-Etcheverry, a professor of urban planning, dean of the architecture faculty, and rector of the university between 1948 and 1956; and José P. Varela-Acevedo, a professor of international law and Uruguayan and Western Hemisphere history, dean of the law faculty, and rector of the university between 1941 and 1948.

Ametzaga began teaching Euskara classes in the university facilities known as the Republic of Argentina Schools (*Escuelas República de Argentina*), located at Calle Colonia 1190 in Montevideo, thereby inaugurating a fruitful academic period of eleven years, after which Dr. José Mendiola continued his efforts for a similar period of time. More than fifty students enrolled in that inaugural session, in April 1944, and the number continued to grow without interruption until 1955. Moreover, in view of the robust success of that first course, a department of Basque studies, under the direction of Bingen Ametzaga, was founded at the Universidad de la República on March 21, 1945. The department offices and what would become over time a large library were located in an old colonial building from the eighteenth century, known as the Port Customs House (*Aduanas del Puerto*) and located at Avenida 18 de Julio 1195 in Montevideo.

It was there that Ametzaga spent ten long years of intense collaboration with the most diverse cultural organizations of the Basque exile community and the most prominent figures of Uruguayan life. The department offices were a gathering place for Adolfo Berro, Justino Jiménez-Arechaga, Eduardo Couture, José M. Fernández-Saldaña, Raúl Montero-Bustamante, Justino Zabala-Muniz, Felipe Ferreiro-Gamio and Salterain Herrera, José Mendiola, Miguel Bañales, Carlos G. Mendilaharzu, Dionisio Garmendia, María Ana Bidegarai-Janssen, Mercedes Iribarren, María and Juana Soto Dendariena, Margarita Gorriti Vaseur, Gabriel Biurrun (Uruguayan consul in Pamplona), Antonio María Barbieri (the archbishop of Montevideo), Lauro Ayestaran (a musician of Basque origin), Francisco Cortabarria, and Ricardo Grille-Eleizalde, among many others.

On the university's initiative, once again, the department took an active part in the 1948 and 1954 international Basque studies conferences (*Congresos Internacionales de Estudios Vascos*). The first of them, held in Bayonne, was attended by Gabriel Biurrun with ten lengthy papers and more than fifty statements of support, including those of university rector José Pedro Varela Acevedo, all the university deans, culture minister Oscar Secco Ellauri, Uruguayan president Luis Conrado Batlle Berres, and practically all the government ministers. Once again, the Uruguayan government confirmed its unconditional support for the Basque people's cause.

Early in 1951, Leopoldo Agorio-Etcheverry, at that time the rector of the university, charged Ametzaga with the creation of a chair of Basque culture, which began to function in March of that year with around fifty students. Classes were held in the old building at Cerrito 73 in Montevideo. At Carlos Vaz-Ferreira's request, the first course took as its textbook the joint translation by Orixe and Ametzaga of the poem *Euskaldunak* (The Basques), which is today considered a classic of twentieth-century Basque literature. As in the case of the chair in Euskara, what had initially started with the idea of a year's specialist course became a professorship that continued to offer classes until 1955, when Ametzaga left Uruguay permanently.

Two years earlier, in 1949, a group of exiles in Iparralde had come up with the idea of organizing an International Day of the Basque Language, *Euskara Eguna*. The celebration was to take place simultaneously in all the Basque centers in Europe and the Americas every year on December 3, the feast day of St Francis Xavier, the patron saint of the Basque language. The money collected at the various Basque centers would be sent to Iparralde for the purpose of promoting the publication of periodicals in Euskara, the creation of Basque-language schools, and in general, all kinds of activities intended to develop the Basque language in Euskal Herria.

The first International Day of the Basque Language (*Euskara Eguna*) was thus celebrated at Montevideo's Basque center, Euskal Erria, on December 3, 1949. Among the many and varied activities organized at the Basque center on that day, it is worth emphasizing the exhibit of Basque books, the cycle of lectures on Basque language and literature, and above all, the organization of a group tasked with planning new activities for subsequent years. In effect, the members of the Universidad de la República's department of Basque studies had the idea of creating within the Montevideo Basque center a group of *Euskaltzaleak* or "lovers of the Basque language." They organized a Basque book club, worked to create a handsome library that would collect all works published in Euskara, and promoted hundreds of cultural events, conversations, colloquia, and even a number of artistic exhibitions, some of them held at SODRE, the Uruguayan government's fine arts institute, or at the Ateneo de Montevideo, which Raúl Montero Bustamante, to whom the Uruguayan Basques of the exile community owe so much, always generously allowed them to use.

The new association's fundamental tasks would be to acquire all works published in Basque by each of its members and, at the same time, to subsidize the publication of at least one work written originally in Euskara each year. It was in this way that in 1950, Ametzaga was commissioned to produce his translation of Shakespeare's *Hamlet,* which would be published two years later, in 1952, in what was the first complete edition of *Hamlet* in Euskara. A year later, again on the feast day of St Francis Xavier, Euskara's patron saint, the Euskaltzaleak group once more called on Ametzaga for a translation, this time of Juan Ramón Jiménez's *Platero y yo,* illustrated in this case with the exquisite drawings of Carlos G. Mendilaharzu. This translation was published by Editorial Florensa in Montevideo in 1953.

Although the Euskaltzaleak group proposed a translation of *Hamlet* to Ametzaga in 1950, Ametzaga had begun work on the play years earlier, in 1945. In fact, he had practically completed half of it in April 1947: "This season I am dedicating my leisure to work of this kind, principally to a translation of *Hamlet,* on which I am already halfway."[29] By summer or at latest by fall 1947, Ametzaga had finished his first, unrevised draft of the translation: "I announce to you that I am already halfway through the fifth and final act of *Hamlet,* but even if I finish it in a few weeks, revising it will still take me two or three months, of course, since I want to do the best I can, and I can only devote myself to these tasks at night. My private affairs, which, fortunately, I believe are going better every day, naturally take up the best part of my time."[30] Nevertheless, the colossal task of making revisions remained to be undertaken. Three different transcriptions of the original translation have survived in more or less complete form, corresponding to

29 Letter from Bingen Ametzaga to Joxe Mari Lasarte, March 12, 1947.
30 Letter from Bingen Ametzaga to Joxe Mari Lasarte, June 27, 1947.

three different time periods. Ametzaga thus began his last round of revisions to his translation of *Hamlet* in late 1950.

Originally, the members of the Euskaltzaleak group at Montevideo's Euskal Erria Basque center wanted to have the book printed in time for Euskara Day in 1951. This turned out to be impossible, despite the fact that the manuscript had been delivered to Andrés Irujo, the director of Buenos Aires's Editorial Ekin, half a year previously, in July 1951, and typesetting had begun in September. The fundamental reason for the delay was that the printers knew no Basque, so that they had to set the type by hand, "letter by letter," with complete uncertainty about what they were doing and no idea of the text, and then put the plates through a lengthy and complex process of correction. Logically, the galleys were full of mistakes, notably increasing the cost of the edition.

Finally, in January 1952, after the final correction of the plates, the work was sent to the print shop, Talleres Gráficos A. Domínguez de La Plata,[31] and in March of that year, Ametzaga received the first proofs or galleys at his house. Despite the corrections to the plates, the book had to go through three rounds of proofs between March and September 1952.[32] On November 22, 1952, Ametzaga received at his house in Montevideo the first copies of the book, which would be publicly introduced by the Euskaltzaleak publishing group at Montevideo's Euskal Erria Basque center on Euskara Day 1952.[33]

Nevertheless, this translation, composed in Uruguay because the man responsible for it was in exile and its publication would have been prohibited in his native land, faced problems from the censorship of Colonel Juan Domingo Perón's Argentine regime, which set up administrative roadblocks to the export of books, so that copies could be sent abroad only if they were labeled "sample without commercial value" or something similar. These obstacles to the sale of the book abroad, along with the censorship process itself, prevented the sale of copies between December 1952 and February 1953.[34] In fact, the only copies that could be sold were the twenty-five that were offered for sale the day the book was introduced at the Montevideo Basque center. A month after

31 Letter from Andrés Irujo to Bingen Ametzaga, August 6, 1952.

32 Letter from Bingen Ametzaga to Pedro Basaldua, July 2, 1953.

33 Letter from Bingen Ametzaga to Andrés Irujo, December 4, 1952.

34 Letter from Andrés Irujo to Bingen Ametzaga, December 4, 1952.

the event, on January 3, 1953, Ametzaga possessed only a single copy, which was shared between the Montevideo Basque center and the Universidad de la República department of Basque studies. The Euskaltzaleak group had a waiting list with seventy-five names, while at Editorial Ekin, Irujo had several hundred copies packed up for export to Europe and the Americas. The situation was not definitively resolved until September 1953, when the book was first offered for sale in a Bilbao bookshop, Librería Villar, for the price of ninety pesetas. The number of orders was such that the press run was quickly exhausted; already in April 1953, the number of subscribers was practically greater than the number of copies, so that Irujo considered reprinting the volume. Nevertheless, financial problems delayed the project again and again.[35]

In contrast to the difficulties that the book's distribution had to overcome, news of its publication spread very rapidly. On the publication date itself, the news was picked up by practically the entire Argentine and Uruguayan domestic press, as well as the most prominent radio stations. On the international level, the translation was noted by press and radio outlets in Paris, Caracas, New York, and London, among others; the New York Association Press; and the BBC. As Irujo, the publisher, commented, "Dear Bingen, I congratulate you. You are having enormous success. . . . On the night of the 3rd [of December 1952] and on the noon news bulletin, the festival and the introduction of your *Hamlet* were mentioned. All the evening papers and others that publish in the morning included reports similar to the enclosed one, which is from *La Razón* on the 3rd. I imagine that you will have seen *La Nación* from the same day there. But there's more. I already told you that I had personally visited the agencies and given them a copy. Well, Association Press, which transmitted the news on Tuesday evening, received a cable from New York yesterday, the 3rd, asking for more details and, in particular, some passages, such as the soliloquy, for example. So there you've got me looking up that part about 'To be or not to be' in order to be able to tell them and send it by telegraph, as the agency did with other details that the people there thought were of interest. But now I need you to give me information about what's been done there and also about whether there was anything in the press about what's

35 Letter from Andrés Irujo to Bingen Ametzaga, April 24, 1953.

been done here. Caracas, New York, and Paris requested the same information."[36]

In February 1953, the publication's resonance, together with the search for copies, remained a live topic. "What a success *Hamlet* is. On January 12, the BBC devoted a special broadcast to your work, which Father Urrutia was supposed to prepare and someone named De la Torre, an engineer in Balmaseda, was supposed to read, and which Hickman, the secretary of the delegation [of the Basque government-in-exile in London], was able to organize with the first copy that arrived in Gondra. The broadcast was satisfactory to all. My own brother [Manuel Irujo] heard it and was pleased, and after the commentary about the work, they were supposed to read some bits of your work in Euskara and others, related to the same text, in English. Think how significant this is. I've submitted an article here and in Mexico, and I imagine that they will also publish it in [the journal] *Euzko Deya* in Paris. We'll write to [the Guatemalan journal] *Euzko Gogoa* today for them to print the report as well."[37]

On the occasion of the coronation of Queen Elizabeth II of England, the Uruguayan Basque delegation in early September 1953 sent a copy of the *Hamlet* translation as a gift. For this presentation copy, "the cover has an artistic illustration, the work of Miss Mireya Oxacelhay. The engraving includes a dedication, fruit of the art of Mr. Carlos Mendilaharsu, framed by the English, Uruguayan, and Basque coats of arms."[38] On the 17th of the same month, the British ambassador to Uruguay, G. M. Warr, in the name of the British Crown, replied with a letter of thanks, stating that "the work in question will be deposited in the Shakespeare Memorial Library in the city of Stratford-on-Avon, as a loan from Her Majesty."[39] It was a small token of recognition and gratitude for the help that the children of the Basque refugee colonies in southern England and Wales received from the British government.

Ametzaga composed and completed translations of three other Shakespeare plays, *Macbeth*, *A Midsummer Night's Dream*, and *Julius Caesar*. None of them would be published during his lifetime, primarily because of the mentioned problem of the lack

36 Letter from Andrés Irujo to Bingen Ametzaga, December 4, 1952.
37 Letter from Andrés Irujo to Bingen Ametzaga, February 5, 1953.
38 *El Plata*, September 1953.
39 Letter from the British Embassy in Montevideo, September 17, 1953.

of expert printers who spoke Euskara in the Americas and the consequent high costs of publication.

Ametzaga's first translation of *Macbeth* preceded his translation of *Hamlet*; in fact, *Macbeth* was his first Shakespeare translation. In January 1941, Ametzaga embarked for the Americas on the *Alsina,* fleeing the Vichy French authorities and the Gestapo itself. As we have had occasion to mention, however, the voyage, which was supposed to take scarcely two weeks, would stretch out for more than a year, until April 1942. From Marseilles, the ship, packed with Basque, Jewish, and Spanish Republican refugees, headed to Dakar. Nevertheless, lacking the indispensable certificate of neutrality, and after approximately three months in Senegal, it had to return to Casablanca, where the passengers were detained in concentration camps by the French authorities, working in collaboration with the pro-Nazi Vichy government. Finally, after several anxious months of waiting, the group of exiles succeeded in departing for Mexico on the *S.S. Quanza,* on November 4, 1941. It would still be another five months, during which the group of refugees spent Christmas in Havana, before Ametzaga arrived in Buenos Aires on board the *Río de la Plata* on April 15, 1942. On the way to Buenos Aires, the *Río de la Plata* was stopped off the northern coast of Brazil by a German submarine, forcing the captain to leave the ship to be interrogated by the German officers on board the submarine. After several anxious hours, the group was able to continue their voyage to the South American continent, from which the vast majority would never return.

One of Ametzaga's fellow passengers on the *Alsina* was Telesforo Monzon, interior minister of the Basque government-in-exile, who was also a poet and writer. The two organized Euskara classes on board and devoted themselves both to writing poetry and, in Ametzaga's case, carrying out small translations for the group's priest, who wanted to celebrate masses in Basque but lacked the necessary texts. This task led Ametzaga to undertake an Euskara translation of *Macbeth,* the English text of which was given to him by another fellow passenger, a Jewish exile. It was the eighth volume of the 1910 Oxford edition, which included three of the four plays that Ametzaga would translate, *Julius Caesar*, *Macbeth,* and *Hamlet.*[40] It was not a coincidence

40 William Shakespeare, *The Complete Works of William Shakespeare,* with a

that Ametzaga decided to translate these three plays, since all of them deal with the death of a tyrant who has obtained the throne by murder, a situation with evident parallels to that of the three tyrants of Western Europe at the time, Franco, Hitler, and Mussolini. The three tragedies give concrete form to the topic of the usurpation of sovereignty and the need to do justice. Ametzaga's translation of *A Midsummer Night's Dream,* found in the second volume of the mentioned Oxford University Press edition, on the other hand, was motivated by very different criteria. In Ametzaga's opinion, this comedy's language was immensely rich from a grammatical and semantic perspective and therefore posed a magnificent challenge to the translator. Ametzaga even translated some of Shakespeare's original songs in verse, as he would also do with the witches' speeches in *Macbeth.*

As Ametzaga commented, he produced the first drafts of his translation of *Macbeth* from English into Euskara and of the works of Pliny the Younger from Latin into Euskara on board the *Alsina* and the *Quanza* and in the Sidi El Ayachi concentration camp: "I do something similar, dedicating myself on board ship to doing translations into Euskara. I translate Latin letters by Pliny, and at the same time, I'm bringing Shakespeare into our national language by way of the characters of *Macbeth.* Without doing anything definitive here at the moment, because of a lack of confidence in the absence of resources with which to resolve some issues, I hope at least to end up with something done and prepared for further work."[41]

Even if Ametzaga's was the first complete translation of *Macbeth* into Euskara, he did have a literary precedent, an abbreviated version of *Macbeth* composed in Basque by the writer Toribio Altzaga and published under the title *Irritza* (Greed) in 1926.[42] Ametzaga's initial translations into Euskara of four plays and various sonnets by Shakespeare between 1941 and 1954 provided the stimulus for the translation of many other works by the same author. Bedita Larrakoetxea translated all of Shakespeare's plays over the course of twenty years, between 1950 and 1970. Among the first works that Larrakoetxea translated into Euskara were

---

General Introduction by Algernon Charles Swinburne (London: Oxford University Press, 1910-11).

41 Letter from Bingen Ametzaga to Manuel Intxausti, August 1941.

42 The complete title is *Irritza Shakespeareren'n macbeth'en gayean, iru egintza eta egintza-aurrean Toribio Alzaga'k euskeratutako antzerkia.*

The Tempest and *Macbeth* (1957), which was published in *Euzko Gogoa,* the journal edited by the writer and translator Jokin Zaitegi in his Guatemalan exile.[43] Starting with these pioneering translations, the translation of Shakespeare's complete works into Euskara has continued without interruption.[44]

From a letter by Ametzaga to the writer Nicolás Ormaetxea, we know that he began translating Shakespeare's *A Midsummer Night's Dream* on board the *Alsina,* between 1941 and 1942, even if he was only able to start making a few notes. Once in Buenos Aires, he completed the first drafts of his first two Shakespeare translations, *Macbeth* and *A Midsummer Night's Dream,* around October 1942. Obviously, the circumstances in which they had been produced meant that they required further rounds of revision, the second of which was finished eleven years later, in April 1953. A year after that, in January 1954, Ametzaga copied out his fourth, revised version of the 1941 original.

In June 1945, he was putting the finishing touches on his first draft of *Julius Caesar,* which he found much simpler to translate, not only because it was his fourth Shakespeare translation, but also, as he said repeatedly in his letters, because of its syntactic structure and semantic content. "As you say at the beginning of your comments, the work is difficult in itself—I confess that it was this that tempted me—but it has the advantage that everything else seems downhill afterward. *A Midsummer Night's Dream* cost me one-twentieth of the effort, and *Julius Caesar*—which I am finishing now—a very great deal less, due to its classical clarity."[45] As Ametzaga wrote to Manuel Irujo, the former justice minister of the Spanish Republic, *Julius Caesar* was a tragedy in the classical style, and the language Shakespeare used was likewise syntactically and semantically plainer. "*Julius Caesar,* due to its severely classical and simple language—something like the antithesis of *Hamlet*—would be the one that would pose the fewest difficulties, and it seems to me that it would be good to start with it. Next would come *Macbeth,* and if the publishers do

43 The translation of *Macbeth* that Larrakoetxea published in *Euzko-Gogoa* in 1957 can be read online at http://www.susa-literatura.eus/emailuak/shakespeare/xexp0500.htm. See also http://andima.armiarma.eus/eugo/eugo38/eugo3812.htm.

44 See some of the online editions of Shakespeare's works in Euskara at http://ekarriak.armiarma.eus/?i=160.

45 Letter from Bingen Ametzaga to Koldo Mitxelena, June 26, 1945.

not get tired of it, I could continue, if God gives me health and good spirits, publishing if not all of Shakespeare, at least his most important works."[46]

In July 1954, he completed the definitive version of his translation of *Julius Caesar.*[47] On October 14, 1954, he completed his translation of *Macbeth,*[48] although he would continue revising it until 1956, fifty years ago now.

Twelve years later, in October 1968, by then in exile in Venezuela, Ametzaga went back to his files and took out his three unpublished Shakespeare translations, *Macbeth, A Midsummer Night's Dream,* and *Julius Caesar,* revising them once more, this time in order to adapt them to the norms established by the Academy of the Basque Language, which reached definitive agreement on the linguistic model for the normalization of Basque at its historic meeting at the monastery of Arantzazu that year: "Today I start my vacation, which I am in great need of, and I'm going to see if I can finish polishing my translations of *Macbeth, Julius Caesar,* and *A Midsummer Night's Dream,* which I had done after *Hamlet,* and get them ready for the press. After having left them sleeping for around fifteen years, it occurred to me a few months ago that after some good updating, that is, avoiding as far as possible everything that might have seemed excessive purism in *Hamlet,* and without falling, as you say, into the opposite extreme of the fashionable butchers of the language [*mordollistas*], whose ideal seems to be to turn Euskara into a patois, it would be worth the trouble to publish them. I've been working on this very lovingly for the last few months, and I have very little left before I'm completely finished. We'll see what can be done."[49]

Nevertheless, he was unable to convert the old translations he had made on board the ship that brought him to the Americas to the new orthography and syntax. Three months later, Bingen Ametzaga died in exile in Caracas, leaving on his desk his three Basque translations of Shakespeare, together with the first lines of two more ambitious translation projects, Dante's *Divine*

46 Letter from Bingen Ametzaga to Manuel Irujo, December 15, 1954.

47 Letter from Bingen Ametzaga to Koldo Mitxelena, June 26, 1954.

48 Letter from Bingen Ametzaga to Manuel Irujo, October 17, 1954.

49 Letter from Bingen Ametzaga to Miguel Pelay Orozco, October 22, 1968.

Comedy[50] from the original Italian and Goethe's *Faust* from the original German.

Ametzaga always hung a small wooden shelf over the doorway of the various houses in which he lived during his thirty-three years in exile. On that shelf, the family kept an old green wicker suitcase, the one with which they had traveled into exile and with which they would return home after the fall of the dictatorship, because when Ametzaga was asked, at a conference held at the Universidad Central in Venezuela, what the destination of his Western Hemisphere exile was, he replied, alluding to Chesterton, that having left his native Algorta for Buenos Aires, by way of Paris, Marseilles, Casablanca, Dakar, Veracruz, and Havana, with stays of twelve and fifteen years in Montevideo and Caracas respectively, his destination was precisely his native Algorta, the place where he wished to die.

Ametzaga was unable to bring his travels to a close, but today there is a plaza overlooking the sea that bears his name opposite one of Algorta's beaches, and his legacy survives: the literary work of a spy who fought in two wars for freedom while translating Shakespeare.

50 Only the first part, the *Inferno*, survives, in a handwritten original.

Preface to *Macbeth* in Basque

It was performed for the first time around 1609 or 1610, but it was written in 1606 and later there were three Macbeths according to some observers: (1) the first play written by Shakespeare, about which we do not know the original date of publication or how widely this was known; (2) the first abridged version of that original work, done by Shakespeare himself, which ran for approximately two hours or less; and (3) an arrangement of that shortened version by someone unknown, perhaps Thomas Middleton? Much has been written about this issue, but that is not our field of concern here. Theater, as we know it today, was not recorded until 1623. And, besides, it would appear that there are several additions to the work.

Shakespeare took this tragedy from Holinshed's book Chronicle of England, Scotland and Ireland (1577). Yet, as usual, our playwright freely uses the declarations provided by the chronicler and how. The fact is that the historical Macbeth is a king and quite different from the character presented to us by the poet. But that is, precisely, what touches our hearts; a man, a living, breathing man with passion and everything else, and not just some kind of role.

The play is short, the shortest of all Shakespeare's dramatic works. It is barely half the length of Hamlet. And the short nature of the work brings with it another distinguishing feature: its vitality. Indeed, this drama has a Greek touch and more than one observer has found within it the influence of the great tragedy and poetry of Achilles. This is a comprehensive tragedy, among the finest there is, a fine example of the power of drama; his characters reveal a supreme humanity and that humanity fits the action perfectly. From beginning to end, the action is taut and composed.

Thought out with great force, simply woven, this is an excellent tragedy characterized by charming beauty. It is a tragedy of ambition, of course, and one rarely sees such murky interiors of a man's heart with their dark erroneous places as here.

Shakespeare's lifetime writings reflect the era of the early seventeenth century onward in that they demonstrate a clear change of that time. That happiness that brought with it jubilant comedies in earlier years disappears; laughter is dismissed from his lips. For whatever reason, for nine or ten years we see that Shakespeare is exploring the triumph of harm, through a demonstration of mankind's downfall, despair, and lack of power. At war with one's very self; the animal within mankind suppressing the good. These are the themes he explores during those years.

In this drama of Macbeth provocation and punishment appear completely concealed; a man driven to destruction and all kinds of sin by the force of being unable to resist. The development and culmination of temptation in Macbeth's mind is worth noting. Goethe equates Macbeth with the Brutus and Hamlet, who like him could not escape being dragged into a trap. It is often also acknowledged that Hamlet and Macbeth are two characters that complement one another: one that is completely incapable of starting anything and another that is never able to stop something he has already started.

Macbeth is the principal character in this play along with his wife. Temptation comes both their ways, in the form of ambition, in other words, at times of yearning it can tempt them in a profound way. But the consequences are very different when it comes to the man and the woman: Macbeth can only live in the fear that has enveloped him, while in his wife, in contrast, we see the effect of a piercing heart. There are villains as well. They become more and more prominent, especially toward the end of Macbeth.

There is emotion, great emotion, in many scenes in the play: in the spectacle of the dagger, in the killings of Duncan and Banquo. In the nocturnal wanderings of Lady Macbeth. And there are the Witches, figures of worldly—or otherworldly—evil.

Macbeth in Basque

Dramatis personae

DUNCAN, king of Scotland
MALCOLM, his son
DONALBAIN, his son
MACBETH, General of the king's army
BANQUO
MACDUFF, nobleman of Scotland.
LENNOX
ROSS
MENTEITH
ANGUS
CAITHNESS
FLEANCE, son to BANQUO
SIWARD, Earl of Northumberland, general of the English forces
YOUNG SIWARD, his son
SEYTON, An officer attending on MACBETH
Son to MACDUFF
An English doctor
A Scottish doctor
A soldier
A porter
An old man
LADY MACBETH
LADY MACDUFF
Gentlewoman attending on LADY MACBETH
HECATE
Three witches
Apparitions
Lords, gentlemen, officers, soldiers, murderers, attendants, and messengers

Dramatis personae

DUNCAN, Eskotelanda'ko errege
MALCOLM, bere semea
DONALBAIN, bere semea
MACBETH, Erregeren gudalburuak
BANQUO
MACDUFF, Eskotelanda'ko aundikiak
LENNOX
ROSS
MENTEITH
ANGUS
CAITHNESS
FLEANCE, BANQUO'ren semea
SIWARD, Northumberland'eko kondea, gudarozte ingelandarraren gudalburua
SIWARD GAZTEA, SIWARD'en semea
SEYTON, MACBETH'en izkillu-ekarle
Mutiko bat, MACDUFF'en semea
Osagille ingelandar bat
Osagille eskotelandar bat
Buruzagi bat
Atezain bat
Agure bat
MACBETH ANDREA
MACDUFF ANDREA
Andre bat, MACBETH ANDREAREN zerbitzaria
HEKATE
Iru sorgin
BANQUO'ren MAMUA ta beste iratxo batzu
Aundikiaren jaunak, guda-agintariak, gudariak, iltzailleak, morroiak eta geznariak.

Act 1

Scene 1

A desert place.
Thunder and lightning. Enter three Witches.

First Witch. When shall we three meet again
In thunder, lightning, or in rain?

Second Witch. When the hurlyburly's done,
When the battle's lost and won.

Third Witch. That will be ere the set of sun.

First Witch. Where the place?

Second Witch. Upon the heath.

Third Witch. There to meet with Macbeth.

First Witch. I come, Graymalkin!

Second Witch. Paddock calls.

Third Witch. Anon.

ALL. Fair is foul, and foul is fair:
Hover through the fog and filthy air.

Exeunt

Scene 2

A camp near Forres.

Alarum within. Enter DUNCAN, MALCOLM, DONALBAIN, LENNOX, with Attendants, meeting a bleeding Sergeant

DUNCAN. What bloody man is that? He can report,

1'go atala

1'go agerraldia

Ordoki soil bat.
Tximist-ostotsak. Iru sorgin sartzen dira.

Lenengo Sorgiña. Noiz dugu irurok birrikusko elkar ortziri,
tximist naiz euri zear?

Bigarren Sorgiña. Burrunba aitzean,
burruka galdu ta irabaztean.

Irugarren Sorgiña. Ori da izango eguzkia etzin baiño lenago.

Lenengo Sorgiña. Zein lekutan?

Bigarren Sorgiña. Otalurrean.

Irugarren Sorgiña. Macbeth arkitu bear dugu an.

Lenengo Sorgiña. Ba-nator. Mari-urdin!

Bigarren Sorgiña. Kunkun'ek deitzen nau.

Irugarren Sorgiña. Berealaxe.

GUZIAK. Itsusia eder da, ederra itsusi.
Egaz daigun laiño ta aize loi gaindi.

Irtetzen dira

2'garren agerraldia

Gudatoki bat Forres'etik urbil.

Turutotsak barruan. DUNCAN erregea, MALCOLM, DONALBAIN, LENNOX sartzen dira beren jarraigoarekin, eta gudari odoldu bat arkitzen dute.

DUNCAN. Nor dugu gizon odoljaio ori? Bere itxuraz badirudi

As seemeth by his plight, of the revolt
The newest state.

MALCOLM. This is the sergeant
Who like a good and hardy soldier fought
'Gainst my captivity. Hail, brave friend!
Say to the king the knowledge of the broil
As thou didst leave it.

Sergeant. Doubtful it stood;
As two spent swimmers, that do cling together
And choke their art. The merciless Macdonwald—
Worthy to be a rebel, for to that
The multiplying villanies of nature
Do swarm upon him—from the western isles
Of kerns and gallowglasses is supplied;
And fortune, on his damned quarrel smiling,
Show'd like a rebel's whore: but all's too weak:
For brave Macbeth—well he deserves that name—
Disdaining fortune, with his brandish'd steel,
Which smoked with bloody execution,
Like valour's minion carved out his passage
Till he faced the slave;
Which ne'er shook hands, nor bade farewell to him,
Till he unseam'd him from the nave to the chaps,
And fix'd his head upon our battlements.

DUNCAN. O valiant cousin! worthy gentleman!

Sergeant. As whence the sun 'gins his reflection
Shipwrecking storms and direful thunders break,
So from that spring whence comfort seem'd to come
Discomfort swells. Mark, king of Scotland, mark:
No sooner justice had with valour arm'd
Compell'd these skipping kerns to trust their heels,
But the Norweyan lord surveying vantage,
With furbish'd arms and new supplies of men
Began a fresh assault.

DUNCAN. Dismay'd not this
Our captains, Macbeth and Banquo?

matxinadaren oraintsuko berriak
eman ditzaigukela.

MALCOLM. Sargenta da,
ni menpetasunetik jarei egitearren gudaro on
eta bulartsu baten gisa gudukatu dana.
Agur, adiskide kementsu ori! Emaiozu
erregeari gudakaren berri, utzi zenun bezela.

Buruzagi. Ezmezean zegon, elkarri besarkatu
ta beren indarra itotzen duten bi igelari antzo.
Macdowald gozagaitzak—matxino izateko
duiña ortarako ba, sortzezko sapokeriz josia
baitago. Eguzki sartaldeko izaroetatik oiñezko
gudari arin eta aztunen laguntza bat artu zuen
eta zoriak, aren auzi madarikatuari parrirri
egiñaz, biurriaren emagaldua zirudian. Guzia
alperrik, ordea, Macbeth bioztunak—izen ori
ongi irabazi du—alaberra gutxietsiz, sarraski
odoltsuez ke zerion ezpata dardaratzen zuela,
kemen'aren kutuna iduri, bide egin baitzuen
gaizkiñaren aurrera eldu arte.
Ez zion eskurik eman ez agurrik egin,
ura txilborretik matraillezurretaraiño
urratu ta aren burua gure almenaen
gaiñean josi zuen arte.

DUNCAN. O, lengusu bioztun ori! Zaldun jator ori!

Buruzagi. Eguzkiak bere ibilbidea asten dun unetik
ontziak ondoratzen dituzten ekaitzak eta tximist
gaizkorrak batzutan sortzen diran bezelaxe, onelaxe ere
atsegiña eskeintzen bide ziguten iturritik atsegabea jaio
zitzaigun. Adizu, Eskotelanda'ko errege orrek, adizu:
kemenaz jantzitako zuzenbideak "kernes" jauzkariari
beren orpoetan ustekaria jartzera beartu zuteneko,
mugon baten billa zebillan Noruai'eko erregeak eraso
zuen berriz, izkillu garbi ta gudari-laguntza berrikin.

DUNCAN. Ta orrek ez al zitun Macbeth eta Banquo
gure gudalburuak bioz-gabetu?

Sergeant. Yes;
As sparrows eagles, or the hare the lion.
If I say sooth, I must report they were
As cannons overcharged with double cracks, so they
Doubly redoubled strokes upon the foe:
Except they meant to bathe in reeking wounds,
Or memorise another Golgotha,
I cannot tell.
But I am faint, my gashes cry for help.

DUNCAN. So well thy words become thee as thy wounds;
They smack of honour both.
[To attendants] Go get him surgeons.

Exit Sergeant, attended

Who comes here?

Enter ROSS

MALCOLM. The worthy thane of Ross.

LENNOX. What a haste looks through his eyes! So should he look
That seems to speak things strange.

ROSS. God save the king!

DUNCAN . Whence camest thou, worthy thane?

ROSS. From Fife, great king;
Where the Norweyan banners flout the sky
And fan our people cold. Norway himself,
With terrible numbers,
Assisted by that most disloyal traitor
The thane of Cawdor, began a dismal conflict;
Till that Bellona's bridegroom, lapp'd in proof,
Confronted him with self-comparisons,
Point against point rebellious, arm 'gainst arm.
Curbing his lavish spirit: and, to conclude,
The victory fell on us.

Buruzagi. Bai,
txolarreak arranoa edo erbiak leoia
bezelaxe.
Egia esateko, aitortu bear dut eztanda bakoitzeko
kañoien antzekoak zirala; ainbeste ugaritu zituzten
beren ukaldiak etsaiaren gaiñean. Zaurien lurrunetan
burua urtatu nai zuten ala beste Golgota bat oroitarazi?
Ezin nezake esan ...
Baiña aultzen naiz; nire zauriak elka ari dira.

DUNCAN. Itzok zauriak bezain goragarriak dauzkak; batzuk eta besteak zintasun-agiriak dituk.
[Laguntzaileei] Ots, eramazute sendatzailleengana.

Buruzagia irtetzen da lagunduta

Nor dator emen?

ROSS sartzen da

MALCOLM. Ross'eko thane jatorra.

LENNOX. Ori gar bizia bere begietan!
Berri aundiak ematera bide dator.

ROSS. Jainkoak lagun dagiola erregeari.

DUNCAN. Nondik zatoz, thane zindo ori?

ROSS. Fife'tik, errege aundi ori,
antxe ikurrin noruaitarrek zerua iraintzen dute ta
gure erria oztutzen beren tolesen aizeaz.
Noruai'ko erregeak berak, gudarozte beldurgarri
batekin eta Cawdar'eko thanea, etoietan
azpisugeena lagun zularik, inka ertsi batetan jarri
giñun; ordun Belona'ren senargaiak, altzairuz
jantzita, aurre egiten dio buruz-buruka, altzairua
altzairuaren aurka, besoa beso bigurriaren aurka,
aren gogo arroputza menperatuz; ta, bukatzeko,
gurea dugu garaipena.

DUNCAN. Great happiness!

ROSS. That now
Sweno, the Norways' king, craves composition:
Nor would we deign him burial of his men
Till he disbursed at Saint Colme's inch
Ten thousand dollars to our general use.

DUNCAN. No more that thane of Cawdor shall deceive
Our bosom interest: go pronounce his present death,
And with his former title greet Macbeth.

ROSS. I'll see it done.

DUNCAN. What he hath lost noble Macbeth hath won.

Exeunt

Scene 3

A heath near Forres. Thunder. Enter the three Witches.

First Witch. Where hast thou been, sister?

Second Witch. Killing swine.

Third Witch. Sister, where thou?

First Witch. A sailor's wife had chestnuts in her lap,
And munch'd, and munch'd, and munch'd: —
"Give me," quoth I:
"Aroint thee, witch!" the rump-fed ronyon cries.
Her husband's to Aleppo gone, master o' the Tiger:
But in a sieve I'll thither sail,
And, like a rat without a tail,
I'll do, I'll do, and I'll do.

Second Witch. I'll give thee a wind.

First Witch. Thou'rt kind.

DUNCAN. Zorion aundia!

ROSS. Bitartean,
Sueno, Noruai'ko erregeak itun bat eskatzen du.
Ez diogu laketu bere illak lurpetzea Kolunbe
deunaren izaroan amar milla dolar ordaindu
ditun arte gure erabateko bearretarako.

DUNCAN. Cawdor'eko thane orrek ez du gure biotzeko
ustea geiago salduko. Zoaz ara, iragarrazu aren eriotz-epaia
ta agur egiozu Macbeth'i ark zun deituraz berberaz.

ROSS. Zure aginduak beteko ditut.

DUNCAN. Irabaz dezala Macbeth zintzoak ark galdua.

Irtetzen dira

3'garren agerraldia

Otalur bat. Ostotsak. Iru Sorgiñak sartzen dira.

Lenengo Sorgiña. Non izan aiz, aizpa?

Bigarren Sorgiña. Txerriak iltzen.

Irugarren Sorgiña. Aizpa, i non?

Lenengo Sorgiña. Itsas-gizon baten emazteak gaztaiñak zeuzkan bere
altzoan eta karraska, karraska, karraska ari zan.
"Emaidan", esan nion,
eta ipur-lodi zikintsuak "Utikan, sorgiña", deadar egin zun.
Aren senarra Alepo'rantz irten da, Katamotza'ren ontziburu; baiña
jarraituko natzaio itsasoz, bae batean,
eta buztan gabeko sagu bat iduri,
ariko naiz, ariko, ariko.

Bigarren Sorgiña. Aize bat emango diñat.

Lenengo Sorgiña. Biotz onekoa aiz.

Third Witch. And I another.

First Witch. I myself have all the other,
And the very ports they blow,
All the quarters that they know
I' the shipman's card.
I will drain him dry as hay:
Sleep shall neither night nor day
Hang upon his pent-house lid;
He shall live a man forbid:
Weary se'nnights nine times nine
Shall he dwindle, peak and pine:
Though his bark cannot be lost,
Yet it shall be tempest-tost.
Look what I have.

Second Witch. Show me, show me.

First Witch. Here I have a pilot's thumb,
Wreck'd as homeward he did come.

Drum within

Third Witch. A drum, a drum!
Macbeth doth come.

ALL. The weird sisters, hand in hand,
Posters of the sea and land,
Thus do go about, about:
Thrice to thine and thrice to mine
And thrice again, to make up nine.
Peace! the charm's wound up.

Enter MACBETH and BANQUO

MACBETH. So foul and fair a day I have not seen.

Irugarren Sorgiña. Eta nik beste bat.

Lenengo Sorgiña. Beste guziak ba-dauzkat.
Putz dagiten aldeak
ta itsastarren mapako
aien bide guziak
dakizkidala, utziko
dut legor, albitz antzo.
Ez gabaz ez egunez
loa ez da esekiko, ez,
aren betazaletik
Biziko da arrozturik
beratzitan beratzi
nekezko astek meazki
ta iñul utziko dute
ta galtzen ez ba-da ere
aren ontzia, ekaitzak
astinduko du, beintzat.
Begira zer daukadan.

Bigarren Sorgiña. Erakuskidan, erakuskidan.

Lenengo Sorgiña. Errira itzultzean ondatu zan
pillotu baten beatza da.

Arratz-otsa barruan

Irugarren Sorgiña. Arratz bat! arratz bat!
Macbeth dator.

GUZIAK. Aizpa aztiok, eskuz-esku,
bein ta berriz birakatu, zeru-
lurren mezulari. Iru birunda iretzako
ta iru birunda niretzat
ta iru birunda geiago
bederatzi ditezentzat.
Isil! Lillura amaitu da.

MACBETH eta BANQUO sartzen dira

MACBETH. Ez dut iñoiz ikusi onen itsusi ta ederra batera dan egunik.

BANQUO. How far is't call'd to Forres?
[They notice the witches]
What are these
So wither'd and so wild in their attire,
That look not like the inhabitants o' the earth,
And yet are on't?
[To the witches]
Live you? or are you aught
That man may question? You seem to understand me,
By each at once her chappy finger laying
Upon her skinny lips: you should be women,
And yet your beards forbid me to interpret
That you are so.

MACBETH. Speak, if you can: what are you?

First Witch. All hail, Macbeth! hail to thee, thane of Glamis!

Second Witch. All hail, Macbeth, hail to thee, thane of Cawdor!

Third Witch. All hail, Macbeth, thou shalt be king hereafter!

BANQUO. Good sir, why do you start; and seem to fear
Things that do sound so fair?
[to the witches]
I' the name of truth,
Are ye fantastical, or that indeed
Which outwardly ye show? My noble partner
You greet with present grace and great prediction
Of noble having and of royal hope,
That he seems rapt withal: to me you speak not.
If you can look into the seeds of time,
And say which grain will grow and which will not,
Speak then to me, who neither beg nor fear
Your favours nor your hate.

First Witch. Hail!

Second Witch. Hail!

Third Witch. Hail!

BANQUO. Zenbat bide dugu
Forres'eraiño?
[Sorgiñak ikusten dute]
Nortzu ditugu oriek, orren igarrak eta orren
zarpailki jantziak, lurreko biztanleak ez
dirudíten eta ala-ere aren gaiñean diran oriek?
[Sorgiñei]
Bizi al zerate ala gizon batek galde egin
dezaioken zerbait zerate? Ulertzen
didazutela dirudi zuetako bakoitzak beatz
zurruna ezpain zimelduetara darama-ta.
Emakumeak bide zerate ta ala-ere zuen
bizarrek ori ziñesten eragozten didate.

MACBETH. Mintza zaitezte, al ba'duzute; zer zaitugu?

Lenengo Sorgiña. Agur, Macbeth! Agur iri, Glamis'eko thane orri!

Bigarren Sorgiña. Agur, Macbeth! Agur iri, Cawdor'eko thane orri!

Irugarren Sorgiña. Agur, Macbeth! geroago errege izango aizen orri!

BANQUO. Nire jaun on ori, zergatik konkortzen zera ta orren ederki
ots egiten duten gauzaen beldur zerala dirudizu?
[Sorgiñei]
Egiaren izenean ametsezkoak ote zerate, ala
azalez agertzen zeratena bera? Agur dagiozute
nire lagun urenari bere oraingo deiturarekin eta
atorkizun atseginkor baten agintza aundiarekin
eta zorarazten dun errege-itxaropen batekin?
Eta niri ez diostazute ezertxo ere? Aldiaren
ernamiñetan sartu ta zein azi agortuko ta zein
mamituko dan aurresan al ba'dezakezute, itz
egidazute niri ere, ez ez zuen eskerrik eskatu ez
zuen gorrotoaren beldurrik ez dudan oni.

Lenengo Sorgiña. Agur!

Bigarren Sorgiña. Agur!

Irugarren Sorgiña. Agur!

First Witch. Lesser than Macbeth, and greater.

Second Witch. Not so happy, yet much happier.

Third Witch. Thou shalt get kings, though thou be none:
So all hail, Macbeth and Banquo!

First Witch. Banquo and Macbeth, all hail!

MACBETH. Stay, you imperfect speakers, tell me more:
By Sinel's death I know I am thane of Glamis;
But how of Cawdor? the thane of Cawdor lives,
A prosperous gentleman; and to be king
Stands not within the prospect of belief,
No more than to be Cawdor. Say from whence
You owe this strange intelligence? or why
Upon this blasted heath you stop our way
With such prophetic greeting? Speak, I charge you.

Witches vanish

BANQUO. The earth hath bubbles, as the water has,
And these are of them. Whither are they vanish'd?

MACBETH. Into the air; and what seem'd corporal melted
As breath into the wind. Would they had stay'd!

BANQUO. Were such things here as we do speak about?
Or have we eaten on the insane root
That takes the reason prisoner?

MACBETH. Your children shall be kings.

BANQUO. You shall be king.

MACBETH. And thane of Cawdor too: went it not so?

BANQUO. To the selfsame tune and words. Who's here?

Enter ROSS and ANGUS

Lenengo Sorgiña. Macbeth baiño txikiagoa ta andiagoa.

Bigarren Sorgiña. Ez orren zoriontsua ta zoriontsuagoa.

Irugarren Sorgiña. Erregeak sortraziko dituk; ez aiz, ordea, errege izango. Agur, Macbeth eta Banquo.

Lenengo Sorgiña. Banquo ta Macbeth, agur!

MACBETH. Geldi zaitezte, mintzaille adikaitzok: esaidazute geiago. Sinel il dala ta ba-dakit Glamis'eko thane naizena, nola, ordea, Cawdor'ekoa? Cawdor'eko thanea bizi da ta orrilloan dagon zalduna dugu; ta errege izatekoari buruz, ori Cawdor izatea baiño ziñesgarriago ez zait. Esaidazute, nondik duzute ezagutza bakan ori? Ala, zergatik otalur soil onen gaiñean bideak isten dizkiguzute, orrelako igarle-agurrekin? Mintza zaitezte, agintzen dizuet.

Sorgiñak itzaltzen dira.

BANQUO. Lurrak ba-ditu anpuluak, urak bezela, ta auek aietakoak dira. Non itzali ote dira?

MACBETH. Eguratsean,eta gorputzadun zirudiena aienatu zan arnasa aizean bezela. Ai gelditu ba'lira.

BANQUO. Baiña mintzatzen geran sorkari oriek ba-ziran emen ala gogamena nastutzen dun azkordinbelarraren erroa jan dugu?

MACBETH. Zure semeak erregeak izango dira.

BANQUO. Ta zu errege izango.

MACBETH. Baita Cawdor'eko thane ere; ez al zuten orrela esan?

BANQUO. Orrelakoxe soiñuz eta mintzoz. Nor da emen?

ROSS eta ANGUS sartzen dira

ROSS. The king hath happily received, Macbeth,
The news of thy success; and when he reads
Thy personal venture in the rebels' fight,
His wonders and his praises do contend
Which should be thine or his: silenced with that,
In viewing o'er the rest o' the selfsame day,
He finds thee in the stout Norweyan ranks,
Nothing afeard of what thyself didst make,
Strange images of death. As thick as hail
Came post with post; and every one did bear
Thy praises in his kingdom's great defence,
And pour'd them down before him.

ANGUS. We are sent
To give thee from our royal master thanks;
Only to herald thee into his sight,
Not pay thee.

ROSS. And, for an earnest of a greater honour,
He bade me, from him, call thee thane of Cawdor:
In which addition, hail, most worthy thane!
For it is thine.

BANQUO. What, can the devil speak true?

MACBETH. The thane of Cawdor lives: why do you dress me
In borrow'd robes?

ANGUS. Who was the thane lives yet;
But under heavy judgment bears that life
Which he deserves to lose. Whether he was combined
With those of Norway, or did line the rebel
With hidden help and vantage, or that with both
He labour'd in his country's wreck, I know not;
But treasons capital, confess'd and proved,
Have overthrown him.

MACBETH. [Aside] Glamis, and thane of Cawdor!
The greatest is behind.
[To ROSS and ANGUS]
Thanks for your pains.

ROSS. Macbeth, erregek atsegiñez artu du zure gurendaren berria, ta matxinoen aurkako liskarrean zure jokabidea onestean arrimenak eta gorespenek berentzen zuten aldizka. Txundioak arturik, ta egun beraren gaiñerakoa gogoraturik, noruaitar izukaitzaren lerroetan ikusten ziñun, zerorrek sortzen zenitun eriotz-irudien beldurrik gabe. Txingorra bezain sarri, mezudunak ba-zetozan alde-erreskan, eta aietako bakoitzak erreiñuko babes aundia izan ziñala ta goraipatu ziñun, zure gorantzak aren oiñetan barreatzen zitutela.

ANGUS. Ba-gatoz gure errege garaiaren izenean zuri eskerrak ematera ta aren aurrera zu bidatzera, ez zu saristatzera.

ROSS. Ta esker aundiago baten aurrerapentzat, agindu nau bere aldetik zuri Cawdor'eko thane izendatzeko. Agur, beraz. thane jator ori, deitura berri orren pean, zure duzu ta.

BANQUO. Zer? Txerrenak egiak esan ditzake?

MACBETH. Crawdor'eko thane bizi da. Zergatik janzten nauzute jesan-soiñekoz?

ANGUS. Cawdor'eko thane izan zana, bizi da oraiño, baiña galdu merezi dun bizi ori epai gogor baten pean dago. Noruaitarrekin ba'zegon ala matxinoa isilleko laguntzaz ta bidez janzten ba'zun ala bere erria ondatzeko biakin batera ari ba'zan ez dakit; baiña ark aitortu ta egiztatu diran etoikeri larriek galtzen dute.

MACBETH. [Berezian] Gladis ta Cawdor'eko thanea!
Ta auen ondoren aundiena . . .
[Goraki, ROSS'i ta ANGUS'i]
Eskerrak zuen nekeengatik.

[To BANQUO]
Do you not hope your children shall be kings,
When those that gave the thane of Cawdor to me
Promised no less to them?

BANQUO. That trusted home
Might yet enkindle you unto the crown,
Besides the thane of Cawdor. But ‘tis strange:
And oftentimes, to win us to our harm,
The instruments of darkness tell us truths,
Win us with honest trifles, to betray’s
In deepest consequence.
[To ROSS and ANGUS]
Cousins, a word, I pray you.

MACBETH. [Aside] Two truths are told,
As happy prologues to the swelling act
Of the imperial theme.
[To ROSS and ANGUS]
—I thank you, gentlemen.
[Aside] This supernatural soliciting
Cannot be ill, cannot be good: if ill,
Why hath it given me earnest of success,
Commencing in a truth? I am thane of Cawdor:
If good, why do I yield to that suggestion
Whose horrid image doth unfix my hair
And make my seated heart knock at my ribs,
Against the use of nature? Present fears
Are less than horrible imaginings:
My thought, whose murder yet is but fantastical,
Shakes so my single state of man that function
Is smother’d in surmise, and nothing is
But what is not.

BANQUO. Look, how our partner’s rapt.

MACBETH. [Aside] If chance will have me king, why, chance may crown me,
Without my stir.

BANQUO. New horrors come upon him,

[BANQUO'ri]
Zure semeak errege izango diralako ustea ez al duzu, Cawdor'eko thanetza eman zidatenak aiek gutxiago agindu ez zieten ezkero?

BANQUO. Ori bete-betean ziñesteak, Cawdor'eko thanetzaren gaiñean koroia itxaroteraiño zirikatu zaitzake. Baiña, aundia da au! Ta sarritan gure galbidera gu eramateko illunpearen esku-ordekoek egiak esaten dizkigute ta lilluratzen gaitute zirtzilleri ez kaltekorrez, ondorengo larrienetara gu narraztutzeko.
[ROSS'i ta ANGUS'i]
Leagusuak, itz bat, mesedez.

MACBETH. [Berezian] Bi aurresan bete dira, errege gaizko drama ekaitsua'ren itzaurre zoriontsuak bezela.
[ROSS'i ta ANGUS'i]
Anitz esker, jaunak.
[Berezian] Izadigaindiko zirika au ba'liteke gaiztoa ez izatea, ta ba'liteke ona ez izatea. Baldin gaiztoa ba'da, zergatik emen dit ondore oneko ezaupide bat egi batekin asi ta? Ba-naiz Cawdor'eko thanea. Ta ona ba'da, zergatik amorea eman, ikaraz nire illeak laztu ta nire biotz tinko au, izaeraren oituraren aurka, saiets-ezurrak jo erazten ditun irudi ikaragarrizko lillura orri? Oraingo beldurrak ez dira irudimenetikoak bezain izugarriak. Nire gogamenak sarraskia oraindik ameskeritzat baizik ez ba'dauka ere, nire arimaren barruti gaisoa ainbesteraiño kordokatzen du ta egimena ustekeritan itotzen da, ta ezer ez da niretzat oraindik ez dana baizik.

BANQUO. Bai arriturik dugula adiskidea! Begirazute.

MACBETH. [Berezian] Alabearrak ni errege izatea agindu ba'du koroatu nazatela nik artan ikustekorik ez dudalarik.

BANQUO. Aginpide berriak orratzetik arako

Like our strange garments, cleave not to their mould
But with the aid of use.

MACBETH. [Aside] Come what come may,
Time and the hour runs through the roughest day.

BANQUO. Worthy Macbeth, we stay upon your leisure.

MACBETH. Give me your favour: my dull brain was wrought
With things forgotten. Kind gentlemen, your pains
Are register'd where every day I turn
The leaf to read them. Let us toward the king.
[To BANQUO]
Think upon what hath chanced, and, at more time,
The interim having weigh'd it, let us speak
Our free hearts each to other.

BANQUO. Very gladly.

MACBETH. Till then, enough. Come, friends.

Exeunt

Scene 4

Forres. The palace.

Flourish. Enter DUNCAN, MALCOLM, DONALBAIN, LENNOX, and Attendants

DUNCAN. Is execution done on Cawdor? Are not
Those in commission yet return'd?

MALCOLM. My liege,
They are not yet come back. But I have spoke
With one that saw him die: who did report
That very frankly he confess'd his treasons,
Implored your highness' pardon and set forth
A deep repentance: nothing in his life
Became him like the leaving it; he died

jantziak bezela dagozkio: ez zazkio ongi etorriko erabiltzeaz baizik.

MACBETH. [Berezian] Datorrena datorrela! Aldiak eta orduak beren bidea egingo dute egun zaillenetan zear!

BANQUO. Macbeth zintzo ori, zure naiaren pean gaude.

MACBETH. Barkatu. nire burumuin kamuts au
gauza erdi aztuetan ari zan. Zaldun argitsuok, zuen
zerbitzuak egunero orrialdea biratuko ditudan
liburu batean idatzita dituzute. Goazen erregegana.
[BANQUO'ri]
Gogoan erabilli gertatua ta geroago,
ura ongi ausnartuta, biotz zabalik itz
egingo diogu elkarri.

BANQUO. Poz-pozik.

MACBETH. Ordurarte, isillik. Goazen, adiskideok.

Irtetzen dira

4'garren agerraldia

Forres. Jauregiko gela bat.

Turutotsa. DUNCAN, MALCOLM, DONALBAIN, LENNOX eta jarraigoa sartzen dira

DUNCAN. Illa da Cawdor? Ortarako joanak ez dira oraindik itzuli?

MALCOLM. Nire jaun ori, ez dute oraindik ostera egin.
Itz egin dut, ordea, ura iltzen ikusi dun norbaitekin.
Esan didanez, bere etoikeriak
zabal-zabal aitortu ta zure
erregetzaren barkamena eskatu
zun, garbai zintzoa erakutsiz.
Ezerk ez zun bere bizia goratu ura

As one that had been studied in his death
To throw away the dearest thing he owed,
As 'twere a careless trifle.

DUNCAN. There's no art
To find the mind's construction in the face:
He was a gentleman on whom I built
An absolute trust.

Enter MACBETH, BANQUO, ROSS, and ANGUS

O worthiest cousin!
The sin of my ingratitude even now
Was heavy on me: thou art so far before
That swiftest wing of recompense is slow
To overtake thee. Would thou hadst less deserved,
That the proportion both of thanks and payment
Might have been mine! only I have left to say,
More is thy due than more than all can pay.

MACBETH. The service and the loyalty I owe,
In doing it, pays itself. Your highness' part
Is to receive our duties; and our duties
Are to your throne and state children and servants,
Which do but what they should, by doing every thing
Safe toward your love and honour.

DUNCAN. Welcome hither:
I have begun to plant thee, and will labour
To make thee full of growing. Noble Banquo,
That hast no less deserved, nor must be known
No less to have done so, let me enfold thee
And hold thee to my heart.

BANQUO. There if I grow,
The harvest is your own.

DUNCAN. My plenteous joys,
Wanton in fulness, seek to hide themselves
In drops of sorrow. Sons, kinsmen, thanes,

utzi dun erak aiña. Daukan gauza maiteenari
deus gutxiko bat bai'litzan uko egitera eriotzean
ikasten ari danaren eraz il da.

DUNCAN. Ez da antzerik
aurpegian gogoaren azalpena
irakurtzeko. Uste osoa jarri
nuen zalduna zan.

MACBETH, BANQUO, ROSS eta ANGUS sartzen dira

Oi, ene lengusu zintzo-zintzo ori! Nire esker
beltzaren ogena astun zitzaidan dagoneko. Orren
urruti egiten duk aurrerantz eta sariaren ega
lasterrena zurrunegia da i atzemateko. Ai ba'u
gutxiago irabazi, eskerron eta sariaren pisua nire
alderantz etzin zedin! Auxe diat bakarrik iri
esateko: ire zorra ordaindu zezakeadan guzia
baiño aundiagoa da.

MACBETH. Zor dizkizudan morroiketa ta zintasuna
beren baitan dute ordaiña. Zuri, errege orri,
dagokizu gure bearkunak onartzea, ta bearkun
oriek jauralki ta lege-erriaren seme ta otseiñak
dituzu, bear dutena besterik egiten ez dutenak zure
maitasarre ta aintzarren al dutena egitean.

DUNCAN. Ongi etorria. Landatzen asi nauk
eta ire azkortze betera eldu zaitezen arte
aleginduko. Banquo zintzo ori, ire irabaziak
ez dira txikiagoak izan eta orobat aldarrikatu
bear dizkiagu. Utzi nazak ene biotz gaiñean
besarka ta estutu zaitzadala.

BANQUO. Artan ernemindu ba'nadi
zure izango duzu uzta.

DUNCAN. Betetasunez mozkortu ta gaiñez egiten
dun nire poz au bere burua negar goibel pean estali
nairik dabil. Seme aide ta aundikiek, eta zuek

And you whose places are the nearest, know
We will establish our estate upon
Our eldest, Malcolm, whom we name hereafter
The Prince of Cumberland; which honour must Not unaccompanied invest him only,
But signs of nobleness, like stars, shall shine
On all deservers. From hence to Inverness,
And bind us further to you.

MACBETH. The rest is labour, which is not used for you:
I'll be myself the harbinger and make joyful
The hearing of my wife with your approach;
So humbly take my leave.

DUNCAN. My worthy Cawdor!

MACBETH. [Aside] The Prince of Cumberland! that is a step
On which I must fall down, or else o'erleap,
For in my way it lies. Stars, hide your fires;
Let not light see my black and deep desires:
The eye wink at the hand; yet let that be,
Which the eye fears, when it is done, to see.

Exit

DUNCAN. True, worthy Banquo; he is full so valiant,
And in his commendations I am fed;
It is a banquet to me. Let's after him,
Whose care is gone before to bid us welcome:
It is a peerless kinsman.

Flourish. Exeunt

Scene 5

Inverness. MACBETH's castle. Enter LADY MACBETH, reading a letter

LADY MACBETH. "They met me in the day of success: and I have
learned by the perfectest report, they have more in
them than mortal knowledge. When I burned in desire

urrengo maillean ditudanok, jakizute Malcolm gure lensemea koroaren jabegai egitea erabaki dugula gaurdanik eta Cumberland'eko erregegai izendatzen dugu. Ez du ura bakarrik nagusitza ontaz jantziko ta, izarrak antzo, aundikitza-deiturak dirdiratuko dute merezidun guzien gaiñean. Orain, goazen Inverness'erantz zurekiko nire zorra aundiago dedin.

MACBETH. Zure morroiketan ematen ez dugun aldia neke zaigu. Nai dut zure geznari nerau izatea ta zure etorreraren berriaz nire emaztearen belarriak poztutzea. Joateko baia eskatzen dizut, ba, aspaldik.

DUNCAN. Nire Cawdor zintzo ori!

MACBETH. [Berezian] Cumberland'eko erregegai! Auxe dut jauzi egin bear dudan mailla ala beaztopatuko naiz, bidea isten dit eta. Izarrok, itzali bitez zuen dirdirak! Ez ditzala zuen argiak ikusi nire naikari beltz eta sakonak. Begiak itxi daitezela eskuaren aurrean. Baiña bete bedi bitartean ura burutzean begiak ikusteko beldur izango dirana.

Irtetzen da

DUNCAN. Egia da, Banquo zindoa, bera oso kementsua da ta ari buruzko gorespenak janari dut; orrits bat dira niretzat. Jarrai gatzazkion guri ongi etorria gertutzeko aurreratzen daiño. Paregabeko aidea dut.

Turutotsa. Irtetzen dira

5'garren agerraldia

Inverness. MACBETH'en gaztelua. MACBETH ANDREA sartzen da eskutitz bat irakurtzen dula

MACBETH ANDREA. "Garaipen egunean irten zitzaizkidan bidera ta ba-dakit eta bide onetik jakin gero, giza-ezagutza baiño geiago dutela.

to question them further, they made themselves air, into which they vanished. Whiles I stood rapt in the wonder of it, came missives from the king, who all-hailed me 'Thane of Cawdor;' by which title, before, these weird sisters saluted me, and referred me to the coming on of time, with 'Hail, king that shalt be!' This have I thought good to deliver thee, my dearest partner of greatness, that thou mightst not lose the dues of rejoicing, by being ignorant of what greatness is promised thee. Lay it to thy heart, and farewell."

Glamis thou art, and Cawdor; and shalt be
What thou art promised: yet do I fear thy nature;
It is too full o' the milk of human kindness
To catch the nearest way: thou wouldst be great;
Art not without ambition, but without
The illness should attend it: what thou wouldst highly,
That wouldst thou holily; wouldst not play false,
And yet wouldst wrongly win: thou'ldst have, great Glamis,
That which cries 'Thus thou must do, if thou have it;
And that which rather thou dost fear to do
Than wishest should be undone.' Hie thee hither,
That I may pour my spirits in thine ear;
And chastise with the valour of my tongue
All that impedes thee from the golden round,
Which fate and metaphysical aid doth seem
To have thee crown'd withal.

Enter a Messenger

What is your tidings?

Messenger. The king comes here to-night.

LADY MACBETH. Thou'rt mad to say it:
Is not thy master with him? who, were't so,
Would have inform'd for preparation.

Messenger. So please you, it is true: our thane is coming:
One of my fellows had the speed of him,

Aiei galde geiago egiteko irrikitzen nengolarik, aize biurtu ziran eta itzali. Ori zala ta txundioak artuta nengola, erregeren mezudunak eldu ziran "Cawdor'eko thane" izenaz agur egin zidatenak. Orixe zan aizpa aztiek niri emandako deitura, geroari buruz gaiñeratzen ere zutela: "Agur iri, errege izango aizen orri!" Ongi iduri zaidan berri au iri ematea, nire aunditasun erkide maite ori, zure poz zatia ez dezazun gal, aztiatzen dizuten izangoaren aunditasuna ez jakiñik. Gorde au biotzean eta agur."

Ba-aiz Glamis eta Cawdor eta agindu diteken guzia izango. Baiña, ire izakeraren beldur nauk; giza-samurtasunen esnez beteegia duk bide laburrena autatzeko. Nai uke aundia izan, irritsa baituk; Baiña lagundu bear dikan gaiztakeria ez. Goraki tirriatzen dukana sainduki gura duk. Ez uke gezurrez jokatu nai, baiña bidegabeko irabazi bat onartuko uke. Nai izango uke, Glamis aundi orrek, "Egin au ni eukitzeko!" oiu egiten dikana, ya aundiago duk ori egiteko beldurra ezin egitearen naia baiño. Ator onara arin, nire adorea belarrietan isuri dezaizun eta alabearrak eta goitiko almenak koroatu iduri auten urrezko oboaren eragozpide guziak askatu ditzadantzat ene mingaiñaren suaz.

Mezudun bat sartzen da

Zer berri dugu?

Mezuduna. Erregea dator ona arratseon.

MACBETH ANDREA. Burutik ago ori esateko. Ire nagusia ez al zegok arekin? Jakitun ipiñiko ninduan bear dana gertutzeko.

Mezuduna. Barkatu, baiña egia da. Gure thanea ba-dator. Nire lagunetato batek

Who, almost dead for breath, had scarcely more
Than would make up his message.

LADY MACBETH. Give him tending;
He brings great news.

Exit Messenger

The raven himself is hoarse
That croaks the fatal entrance of Duncan
Under my battlements. Come, you spirits
That tend on mortal thoughts, unsex me here,
And fill me from the crown to the toe top-full
Of direst cruelty! make thick my blood;
Stop up the access and passage to remorse,
That no compunctious visitings of nature
Shake my fell purpose, nor keep peace between
The effect and it! Come to my woman's breasts,
And take my milk for gall, you murdering ministers,
Wherever in your sightless substances
You wait on nature's mischief! Come, thick night,
And pall thee in the dunnest smoke of hell,
That my keen knife see not the wound it makes,
Nor heaven peep through the blanket of the dark,
To cry 'Hold, hold!'

Enter MACBETH

Great Glamis! worthy Cawdor!
Greater than both, by the all-hail hereafter!
Thy letters have transported me beyond
This ignorant present, and I feel now
The future in the instant.

MACBETH. My dearest love,
Duncan comes here to-night.

LADY MACBETH. And when goes hence?

MACBETH. To-morrow, as he purposes.

aurrea artu dio ta eldu berri da bere mezua
emateko bear dun arnasa ez daukana.

MACBETH ANDREA. Lagun akio.
Berri aundiak ekartzen zizkiguk.

Mezuduna irtetzen da

Belea bera ere erlastutzen da Duncan'en zorigaiztoko sarrera nire dorre-ortzen pean iragartzen dula bere karrankaz. Zatozkidate asmo eriotzegiñen morroi zeraten mamuok, kuntzez aldatu nazazute, ta burutik beatzera bete nazazute, ankerkeri gozagaitzenaz gaiñez egin dezadala egizute. Gogortu ezazute nire odola; itxi ezadazute errukirako edozein sarrera ta igarobide, izaerazko garbai-biozkada batek ere nire asmo gaiztoa kezkarazi ez dezantzat, ura ta egintzaren artean jarrita. Zatozte nire amaugatzetara ta beazun biurtu nire esnea, zuek, sarraskiaren morroiok, tankera ikus-ezin pean gizonen gaitzari begira zaudeten edonondik. Zatoz, gau itsu ori, ta il-jantzi zaitez sulezko ke mordo itzaltsuenaz. Nire sastakai zorrotzak ez dezala egiten dun zauria, ta zeruak illunpeen estalkian zear niri kuzkuzka, egin dezaidakela oiukatu: "Aski, aski!"

MACBETH sartzen da

Glamis aundi ori, Cawdor zintzo ori,
biok baiño aundiagoa iragarri
agurraren arauz! Ire eskutitzak
oraingo illun au baiño aruntzago
eraman eta geroaz atsegintzen nauk.

MACBETH. Ene maitea,
Duncan gau ontan dator.

MACBETH ANDREA. Eta noiz joateko emendik?

MACBETH. Biar; ori da bere asmoa.

LADY MACBETH. O, never
Shall sun that morrow see!
Your face, my thane, is as a book where men
May read strange matters. To beguile the time,
Look like the time; bear welcome in your eye,
Your hand, your tongue: look like the innocent flower,
But be the serpent under't. He that's coming
Must be provided for: and you shall put
This night's great business into my dispatch;
Which shall to all our nights and days to come
Give solely sovereign sway and masterdom.

MACBETH. We will speak further.

LADY MACBETH. Only look up clear;
To alter favour ever is to fear:
Leave all the rest to me.

Exeunt

Scene 6

Before MACBETH's castle.

Hautboys and torches. Enter DUNCAN, MALCOLM, DONALBAIN, BANQUO, LENNOX, MACDUFF, ROSS, ANGUS, and attendants.

DUNCAN. This castle hath a pleasant seat; the air
Nimbly and sweetly recommends itself
Unto our gentle senses.

BANQUO. This guest of summer,
The temple-haunting martlet, does approve,
By his loved mansionry, that the heaven's breath
Smells wooingly here: no jutty, frieze,
Buttress, nor coign of vantage, but this bird
Hath made his pendent bed and procreant cradle:
Where they most breed and haunt, I have observed,
The air is delicate.

MACBETH ANDREA. Oi, iñoiz ere ez du eguzkiak biar ori ikusiko! Zure aurpegia, ene thane ori, hauza bakanak irakurri ditekezan liburua da. Gizarteari iruzur egiteko gizartea bezela iruditu. Eramazu ongietorria begietan, mingaiñean, eskuetan eta lore bakun baten antzean agertu; baiña izan zaitez lore orren azpian ezkutatzen dan sugea. Datorrenaz ari gaitezan. Utzi nire gain gau ontako egiteko aundia; ark emango dizkie gure geroko egunei agintaritza ta al izate goiena.

MACBETH. Gero mintzatuko gera berriz.

MACBETH ANDREA. Begi argi erabilli. Aurpegiaren besteratzeak beldurra erakusten du. Gaiñerakoa utzazu nire bizkar.

Irtetzen dira

6'garren agerraldia

MACBETH'en gazteluaren aurrean.

Zaamiolak eta zuziak. DUNCAN, MALCOLM, DONALBAIN, BANQUO, LENNOX, MACDUFF, ROSS, ANGUS eta jarraigoa sartzen dira.

DUNCAN. Leku zoragarrian dago gaztelu au. Eguratsa, legun eta gozoa, atsegingarri zaie, berez, zentzunei.

BANQUO. Uda-arrotz eta jauretxe-biztanle dan enarak, bere aterpe maiteaz erakusten digu zeruetako arnasa goxoki lurrinkatzen ari dala emen. Ez dago txoritxo onek bere oe zintzilikaria ta seaska umekorra egin ez dun erlaizik, ez arrapalik, ez txoko egokirik. Oartu naiz ura geien bizi ta maiz biltzen dan lekuan eguratsa biguiña dala.

Enter LADY MACBETH

DUNCAN. See, see, our honour'd hostess!
The love that follows us sometime is our trouble,
Which still we thank as love. Herein I teach you
How you shall bid God 'ild us for your pains,
And thank us for your trouble.

LADY MACBETH. All our service
In every point twice done and then done double
Were poor and single business to contend
Against those honours deep and broad wherewith
Your majesty loads our house: for those of old,
And the late dignities heap'd up to them,
We rest your hermits.

DUNCAN. Where's the thane of Cawdor?
We coursed him at the heels, and had a purpose
To be his purveyor: but he rides well;
And his great love, sharp as his spur, hath holp him
To his home before us. Fair and noble hostess,
We are your guest to-night.

LADY MACBETH. Your servants ever
Have theirs, themselves and what is theirs, in compt,
To make their audit at your highness' pleasure,
Still to return your own.

DUNCAN. Give me your hand;
Conduct me to mine host: we love him highly,
And shall continue our graces towards him.
By your leave, hostess.

Exeunt

Scene 7

MACBETH's castle.

Hautboys and torches. Enter a Sewer, and divers Servants with dishes and service, and pass over the stage. Then enter MACBETH

MACBETH ANDREA sartzen da

DUNCAN. Ikus, ikus! Gure arroztiar zintzoa! Gure jarrai dabillen maitasuna nekagarri zaigu batzutan; esker diogu ala ere, maitasuna dalako. Onekin esan nai dizut Jainkoari eskatu dezaiozula gu sariztatzeko zuen nekeengatik, ta eskertsu zakizkigula emango dizkigun naigabeak dirala ta.

MACBETH ANDREA. Gure morroi-lan guziak, bikundu ta berrikatuak ere, opari urri ta bakuna izango litzake, zuk, Errege orrek, gure etxea bete duzun oore aundi ta zabal orien aldean. Zure lengo onegiñak eta aiei oraintsu gaiñeratu dizkiezun eskerrak dirala ta zure padarrak gaituzu.

DUNCAN. Nun da Cawdor'eko thanea? Orpoz-orpo jarraitu gatzazkio aren ornitzaillea izateko asmoz; zaldizko ona dugu, ordea, ta aren maitasun aundiak, bere aztala bezain zorrotza, gu baiño len etxeratu zun. Ostatu andre eder, uren ori, zure arrotz gaituzu gau ontan.

MACBETH ANDREA. Zure otseiñek, diran eta daukaten guzia gordekizun bezela baiño ez dute, ta on zaizunean zuri kontu emateko gertu daude, zure duzuna berriz ar dezazun.

DUNCAN. Emaidazu esku ori: bida nazazu nire ostatu-emailleagana. Maite-maite dugu ta jarraituko gera gure ontarteak ari erakusten. Zure baimenarekin, ostatu andrea.

Irtetzen dira

7'garren agerraldia

Gaztelua. Zaamiolak eta zuziak.

Mai-mutil bat sartu ta ba-doa agertokian zear, zenbait otsein azpil eta maiontzikin darraizkiola. Bereala MACBETH

MACBETH. If it were done when 'tis done, then 'twere well
It were done quickly: if the assassination
Could trammel up the consequence, and catch
With his surcease success; that but this blow
Might be the be-all and the end-all here,
But here, upon this bank and shoal of time,
We'ld jump the life to come. But in these cases
We still have judgment here; that we but teach
Bloody instructions, which, being taught, return
To plague the inventor: this even-handed justice
Commends the ingredients of our poison'd chalice
To our own lips. He's here in double trust;
First, as I am his kinsman and his subject,
Strong both against the deed; then, as his host,
Who should against his murderer shut the door,
Not bear the knife myself. Besides, this Duncan
Hath borne his faculties so meek, hath been
So clear in his great office, that his virtues
Will plead like angels, trumpet-tongued, against
The deep damnation of his taking-off;
And pity, like a naked new-born babe,
Striding the blast, or heaven's cherubim, horsed
Upon the sightless couriers of the air,
Shall blow the horrid deed in every eye,
That tears shall drown the wind. I have no spur
To prick the sides of my intent, but only
Vaulting ambition, which o'erleaps itself
And falls on the other.

Enter LADY MACBETH

How now! what news?

LADY MACBETH. He has almost supp'd: why have you left the chamber?

MACBETH. Hath he ask'd for me?

LADY MACBETH. Know you not he has?

MACBETH. Ura egin eta geiagorik ez ba'lego! Obe huke ordun berandu gabe ura egitea. Sarraskiak bere ondatza galerazi ta aren amaiaz ondore ona eskuratu al ba'leza! Ukaldi ori guzi-guzia emen bear ba'litz, oraingo biziaren ondarpilla ta ondo garaiaren gaiñean etortzekoa arriskatuko genuke. Onelakoetan, ordea, ementxe dugu epaia ta gure irakaspen odoltsuak beren asmatzaillearen aurka itzultzen dira. Zuzenbideak, esku berdiñez, naastu dugun edontziaren edena eskaintzen die gero ezpaiñei. Segurantza bikoitz baten pean dago emen. Lenik, aren aide ta menpeko naiz: bi zer indartsu sarraskiaren aurka. Gaiñera, aren ostatatzaillea legez, aren iltzailleari atea itxi bearko nioke, ez neronek sastakaia artu. Azkenik orrako Duncan orrek bere eskubidea orren goxoki erabilli du, bere egin-bideetan ain garbia izan da ta bere onindarrek ots egingo lukete aingeruen antzera turuta mintzoz aren kentzearen egintza gaiztoaren aurka.
Ta errukiak aize-erauntsian larrugorri zaldikatzen dan aur jaio berri bat iduri, edo aizearen zaldi ikus-eziñan egaetan eramana dan kerubin bat antzo, egintza ikaragarria agiri egingo luke begi guzien aurrean, negar malkoek aizea ito arte. Ez daukat beste aztalik nire asmoaren alboak akullutzeko nire aundinai gartsua baizik, geiegi jauzi ta beste aldera erortzen dana.

MACBETH ANDREA sartzen da

Oles, zer berri?

MACBETH ANDREA. Aparia bukatzen dago. Zergatik utzi duzu gela?

MACBETH. Galdetu al du nire berri?

MACBETH ANDREA. Ez al dakizu?

MACBETH. We will proceed no further in this business:
He hath honour'd me of late; and I have bought
Golden opinions from all sorts of people,
Which would be worn now in their newest gloss,
Not cast aside so soon.

LADY MACBETH. Was the hope drunk
Wherein you dress'd yourself? hath it slept since?
And wakes it now, to look so green and pale
At what it did so freely? From this time
Such I account thy love. Art thou afeard
To be the same in thine own act and valour
As thou art in desire? Wouldst thou have that
Which thou esteem'st the ornament of life,
And live a coward in thine own esteem,
Letting "I dare not" wait upon "I would,"
Like the poor cat i' the adage?

MACBETH. Prithee, peace:
I dare do all that may become a man;
Who dares do more is none.

LADY MACBETH. What beast was't, then,
That made you break this enterprise to me?
When you durst do it, then you were a man;
And, to be more than what you were, you would
Be so much more the man. Nor time nor place
Did then adhere, and yet you would make both:
They have made themselves, and that their fitness now
Does unmake you. I have given suck, and know
How tender 'tis to love the babe that milks me:
I would, while it was smiling in my face,
Have pluck'd my nipple from his boneless gums,
And dash'd the brains out, had I so sworn as you
Have done to this.

MACBETH. If we should fail?

LADY MACBETH. We fail!
But screw your courage to the sticking-place,
And we'll not fail. When Duncan is asleep—

MACBETH. Ez dugu urrutirago joan bear aziorrazi ontan. Oraintsu bete nau ospez eta urrezko aipu bat irabazi dut guzitariko lagunen artean, eraman nai nukena aren dirdira berriz. Ez ura astandu onen laster.

MACBETH ANDREA. Mozkorturik zegon, beraz, janzten ziñan itxaropena? Lokartu al da gero ta orain itzartzen al da zurbil ta muskerrik begiztatzeko ain arroki so egin zeniona? Oraidanik orrelakotzat artuko diat ire maitasuna. Beldur al aiz ire egitez ta kemenez, gurariz aizena bera izateko? Bizitzaren edergaillutzat jotzen dukana euki nai uke ta ire oniritzian koldar bat antzo bizi izan, "Ez dut bekokirik" bat "Nai nuke" aren atzetik joan dedilla utziz, arako katu gaiso ura bezela?

MACBETH. Isili, arren!
Gizona ausartu dukan edozertara ausartzen nau;
geiagora ausartzen dukana ez dun gizon.

MACBETH andrea. Zein bidutzi izan duk, ba, asmo ori niri agertu eragin dikana? Artarako bekoki zuanean ordun gizona intzan eta intzana baiño areago izateko gizona baiño geiago izan bear. Ez aldia, ez lekua, ez ituan ordun agertzen. eta ala ere ik biok sortu nai. Orain berenez sortuak dituk eta egokiera orretxek ezereztatzen au. Titi eman diat eta badakiat ugatza edoskitzen zidakan umea maitatzea dukan gozoa. Ala ere, nire begi aurrean parrezirriz ari uala, aren ezur gabeko oietatik nire erroa idoki ta burumuiña zapart eragingo nioan zin egin ba'nu, ik au bezela.

MACBETH. Baldin uts egin ba'geneza?

MACBETH ANDREA. Guk uts egin!
Eramazu zure kemena aren tinka-punturaiño ta ez dugu uts egingo. Duncan lokartu dedinean—ta

Whereto the rather shall his day's hard journey
Soundly invite him—his two chamberlains
Will I with wine and wassail so convince
That memory, the warder of the brain,
Shall be a fume, and the receipt of reason
A limbeck only: when in swinish sleep
Their drenched natures lie as in a death,
What cannot you and I perform upon
The unguarded Duncan? what not put upon
His spongy officers, who shall bear the guilt
Of our great quell?

MACBETH. Bring forth men-children only;
For thy undaunted mettle should compose
Nothing but males. Will it not be received,
When we have mark'd with blood those sleepy two
Of his own chamber and used their very daggers,
That they have done't?

LADY MACBETH. Who dares receive it other,
As we shall make our griefs and clamour roar
Upon his death?

MACBETH. I am settled, and bend up
Each corporal agent to this terrible feat.
Away, and mock the time with fairest show:
False face must hide what the false heart doth know.

Exeunt

gaurko bidaldi neketsuak lozorrora deituko dio, nunbait—aren bi gela-zaiñak jan-edanaz azpiratuko ditut, aien oroimena, burumuiñaren begirari ori, ke utsa biurtzeraiño ta adimenaren ontzia iragazki bat. Beren bizi indarra edariz okituta, eriotzarenaren antzeko urde-lo batean pulunpatu ditezenean, zer ez dezakegu zuk eta biok bururatu Duncan laguntza-gabearekin? Zer ez diegu ezarriko aren belaki antzeko menpekoai? Nori emango zaio sarraski aundi orren obena?

MACBETH. Ez erditu semeak baizik! Ire adore izugarriak arrak besterik ez baititzake sortu. Aren bi gelazain lokartuak odolez zikindu ta aien sastakaiak berak erabilli ditzagun ezkero, nork ez din egitzat artuko aiek egin zitenala?

MACBETH ANDREA. Nork ote du besterik ziñetsiko, aieneka ta deitoraka ari gaitezenean eriotza dala ta?

MACBETH. Etsia nago, ta nire indar guziakin zailduko naiz egiteko ikaragarri ortarako. Goazen, eta iruzurra sartu dezaiogun munduari iduri atsegingarrienaz. Aurpegi gezurtiak biotz gezurtiak dakiana estaldu bear du.

Irtetzen dira

Act 2

Scene 1

Court of MACBETH's castle.

Enter BANQUO, and FLEANCE bearing a torch before him

BANQUO. How goes the night, boy?

FLEANCE. The moon is down; I have not heard the clock.

BANQUO. And she goes down at twelve.

FLEANCE. I take't, 'tis later, sir.

BANQUO. Hold, take my sword. There's husbandry in heaven;
Their candles are all out. Take thee that too.
A heavy summons lies like lead upon me,
And yet I would not sleep: merciful powers,
Restrain in me the cursed thoughts that nature
Gives way to in repose!

Enter MACBETH, and a Servant with a torch

Give me my sword.
Who's there?

MACBETH. A friend.

BANQUO. What, sir, not yet at rest? The king's a-bed:
He hath been in unusual pleasure, and
Sent forth great largess to your offices.
This diamond he greets your wife withal,
By the name of most kind hostess; and shut up
In measureless content.

MACBETH. Being unprepared,
Our will became the servant to defect;
Which else should free have wrought.

2'garren atala

1'go agerraldia

Inverness. Gaztelu barruko bailla.

BANQUO ta FLEANCE sartzen dira, zuzi bat daramatela

BANQUO. Gau berandua al diagu, mutil?

FLEANCE. Illargia estali da, ta ez dut erlojua entzun.

BANQUO. Amabietan sartzen da.

FLEANCE. Beranduago da, nik uste.

BANQUO. Tori, ar zak nire ezpata. Zerua xuur zegok gau ontan; bere arkai guziak itzali dituk. Ar zak au ere (Itoltza ta sastakaia ematea dizkio). Beruna bezain astuneko logura diat nire gaiñean, eta ala ere, ez nuke lorik egin nai. Aldun errukitsuok, ezi itzazute nigan izaerak lotan leku egiten ziekan gogoeta madarikatuak!

MACBETH eta Otsein bat sartzen dira, zuzi batekin

Emaidak ezpata.
Nor da?

MACBETH. Adiskide bat.

BANQUO. Zer, jauna, oraiño etzan gabe?
Errege oera da. Oi ez bezelako olde onean
egon da ta emaitz aundiak: egin dizkie zure
otseiñei. Arribizi onekin, berriz, agur egiten
dio zure emazteari, ostatu-andre onbegienari
bezela. Poz-pozik amaitu du eguna.

MACBETH. Gerturik ez geundela,
gure nai ona gutxitarako izan da;
bestela bide zabala artuko zun.

BANQUO. All's well.
I dreamt last night of the three weird sisters:
To you they have show'd some truth.

MACBETH. I think not of them:
Yet, when we can entreat an hour to serve,
We would spend it in some words upon that business,
If you would grant the time.

BANQUO. At your kind'st leisure.

MACBETH. If you shall cleave to my consent, when 'tis,
It shall make honour for you.

BANQUO. So I lose none
In seeking to augment it, but still keep
My bosom franchised and allegiance clear,
I shall be counsell'd.

MACBETH. Good repose the while!

BANQUO. Thanks, sir: the like to you!

Exeunt BANQUO and FLEANCE

MACBETH. [To Servant] Go bid thy mistress, when my drink is ready,
She strike upon the bell. Get thee to bed.

Exit Servant

Is this a dagger which I see before me,
The handle toward my hand? Come, let me clutch thee.
I have thee not, and yet I see thee still.
Art thou not, fatal vision, sensible
To feeling as to sight? or art thou but
A dagger of the mind, a false creation,
Proceeding from the heat-oppressed brain?
I see thee yet, in form as palpable
As this which now I draw.

BANQUO. Ongi dago dana.
Bart Aizpa Aztiakin egin dut amets.
Egiti samarrak gertatu dira zuri buruz.

MACBETH. Ez dut aietaz gogoeta egiten onezkero.
Ala ere, aukerako ordu betea izan
dezagunean, ura eman genezake azi-orrazi
orretzaz mintzatzen, on ba'zaizu.

BANQUO. Nai dezazunean.

MACBETH. Baldin aldia datorrenean nire iritziko
ba'zaitut . . . omena irabaziko duzu.

BANQUO. Baldin galdu ez ba'dezat ura
aunditzeko billatzean eta biotza garbi ta
zintasuna argi gorde-ezkero, aolkuak
entzungo ditut.

MACBETH. Ongi lo egin anartean.

BANQUO. Anitz esker, jauna; bai zuk ere.

BANQUO eta FLEANCE irtetzen dira

MACBETH. [Otseiñari] Esaiok ire
ugazandreari nire edaria gerturik zegokanean
txiliña jo dezala. Oe oera.

Otseiña irtetzen da

Sastakai bat al da nire aurrean dakusadan
ori, kiderra nire eskurantz? Ator atzitu
zaitzadan. Ez aukat eta ala ere beti akust. Ez
al aiz, ikuskari gaizto ori, ukumenari
ikusmenari bezain oargarria? Ala
gogamenezko sastakai bat besterik ez aut,
burumuin sukardun batetiko gezur sorpena?
Oraiño ba-akust, orain zorrotik ateratzen
duadan au bezain ukigaia dirudikala. Ik

Thou marshall'st me the way that I was going;
And such an instrument I was to use.
Mine eyes are made the fools o' the other senses,
Or else worth all the rest; I see thee still,
And on thy blade and dudgeon gouts of blood,
Which was not so before. There's no such thing:
It is the bloody business which informs
Thus to mine eyes. Now o'er the one halfworld
Nature seems dead, and wicked dreams abuse
The curtain'd sleep; witchcraft celebrates
Pale Hecate's offerings, and wither'd murder,
Alarum'd by his sentinel, the wolf,
Whose howl's his watch, thus with his stealthy pace.
With Tarquin's ravishing strides, towards his design
Moves like a ghost. Thou sure and firm-set earth,
Hear not my steps, which way they walk, for fear
Thy very stones prate of my whereabout,
And take the present horror from the time,
Which now suits with it. Whiles I threat, he lives:
Words to the heat of deeds too cold breath gives.

A bell rings

I go, and it is done; the bell invites me.
Hear it not, Duncan; for it is a knell
That summons thee to heaven or to hell.

Exeunt

Act 2, Scene 2

The same.

Enter LADY MACBETH

LADY MACBETH. That which hath made them drunk hath made me bold;
What hath quench'd them hath given me fire.
Hark! Peace!
It was the owl that shriek'd, the fatal bellman,
Which gives the stern'st good-night. He is about it:

erakusten didak artu bear diadan bidea ta erabilli bear diadan izkillua! Nire begiok beste zentzumenen josta illu dira, ala aiek guziak aiña balio ditek, ba-akust beti ta ire kirten eta aboan lenago ez zegozean odol tantak. Baiñan ez duk orrelakorik. Nire asmo odoljarioa duk nire begi aurrean itxura ortaz janzten dukana . . . Orain lurbillaren erdian izadiak illa zirudik eta amets gaiztoak iruzur egiten ziotek itzalkari artean zetzakan loari. Sorgiñak Hekate zurbillarin jauresketan ari dituk eta eriotzegille zimela bere begiraria dukan otsoaren marruak esnatua, Tarkin baten urrats isil eta arrapakeriz, ba-zioak itzalgaizka, iratxo bat iduri, bere jo-mugara. I, lur tinko, sendo orrek ez entzun nire oinkadak, nondik nai ziaztikala. Ire arriek ere nire bidea ager-erazi ta orduari zegokiokan laztura isilla aienatu ez dezaten beldurrez. Ni eskainka ari naukan artean, ura bizi duk. Itzen atsak egintza beroa oztutzen dik.

Joale batek jotzen du

Ba-natxiak eta egiña duk; joaleak deitzen natxiok. Ez entzun, Duncan, zerura ala inpernura dei egiten dikan joale-otsa.

Irtetzen dira

2'garren atala. 2'garren agerraldia

Lengo lekua.

MACBETH Andrea sartzen da

MACBETH ANDREA. Oriek ordierazi ditunak ausartarazi nau ni.
Oriek izungi ditunak, su eman dit . . .
Entzun! Isil! Untza da garrasi egin
duna, bere gabon (makurrena)
ematen dun joale-jotzaille gaiztoa.
Egin bide du. Ateak zabalik dagoz ta

The doors are open; and the surfeited grooms
Do mock their charge with snores: I have drugg'd
their possets,
That death and nature do contend about them,
Whether they live or die.

MACBETH. [Within] Who's there? what, ho!

LADY MACBETH. Alack, I am afraid they have awaked,
And 'tis not done. The attempt and not the deed
Confounds us. Hark! I laid their daggers ready;
He could not miss 'em. Had he not resembled
My father as he slept, I had done't.

Enter MACBETH

My husband!

MACBETH. I have done the deed. Didst thou not hear a noise?

LADY MACBETH. I heard the owl scream and the crickets cry.
Did not you speak?

MACBETH. When?

LADY MACBETH. Now.

MACBETH. As I descended?

LADY MACBETH. Ay.

MACBETH. Hark!
Who lies i' the second chamber?

LADY MACBETH. Donalbain.

MACBETH. [Looking on his hands] This is a sorry sight.

LADY MACBETH. A foolish thought, to say a sorry sight.

gelazaiñak, ardoz aseta, zurrunkan ari diraberen eginbearrari irriz. Aien edarian droga ain eraginkorra jarri dut eta bizia ta eriotza norgeiagoka ari dira aiengan.

MACBETH. [Barruan] Nor da or? Zer? Oles!

MACBETH ANDREA. Esnatu ote diran eta uts egin ote dugun beldur naiz. Saioak galtzen gaitu ez egiteak. Entzun! Aien sastakaiak gerturik utzi nitun; ikusi izan bear ditu. Neronek egingo nun nire aita lokartua oroitarazi baldin ez ba'lit.

MACBETH sartzen da

Nire senarra!

MACBETH. Egitekoa egiña dun. Ez al duzu zaratarik entzun?

MACBETH ANDREA. Untzaren garrasia ta kilkerren soiñua. Ez al duzu itz egin?

MACBETH. Noiz?

MACBETH ANDREA. Arestian.

MACBETH. Jexten nintzanean?

MACBETH ANDREA. Bai.

MACBETH. Adi zan!
Nor zetzan bigarren gelan?

MACBETH ANDREA. Donalbain.

MACBETH. [Bere eskuai begira] Au ikuskizun negargarria!

MACBETH ANDREA. Zorakeria duk ikuskizun negargarria esatea.

MACBETH. There's one did laugh in's sleep, and one cried "Murder!"
That they did wake each other: I stood and heard them:
But they did say their prayers, and address'd them
Again to sleep.

LADY MACBETH. There are two lodged together.

MACBETH. One cried "God bless us!" and "Amen" the other;
As they had seen me with these hangman's hands.
Listening their fear, I could not say "Amen,"
When they did say "God bless us!"

LADY MACBETH. Consider it not so deeply.

MACBETH. But wherefore could not I pronounce "Amen"?
I had most need of blessing, and "Amen"
Stuck in my throat.

LADY MACBETH. These deeds must not be thought
After these ways; so, it will make us mad.

MACBETH. Methought I heard a voice cry "Sleep no more!
Macbeth does murder sleep", the innocent sleep,
Sleep that knits up the ravell'd sleeve of care,
The death of each day's life, sore labour's bath,
Balm of hurt minds, great nature's second course,
Chief nourisher in life's feast,—

LADY MACBETH. What do you mean?

MACBETH. Still it cried "Sleep no more!" to all the house:
"Glamis hath murder'd sleep, and therefore Cawdor
Shall sleep no more; Macbeth shall sleep no more."

LADY MACBETH. Who was it that thus cried? Why, worthy thane,
You do unbend your noble strength, to think
So brainsickly of things. Go get some water,
And wash this filthy witness from your hand.
Why did you bring these daggers from the place?

MACBETH. Batak bere loan parre egin ziñan; besteak "Eriotzegille" ots egin dik ta biek iratzarri ditek elkar. Geldi ta adi nengonan ni; baiña otoiak esan eta lokartu itunan berriro.

MACBETH ANDREA. Biak gela batean zegozen.

MACBETH. Batak oiu egin ziñan "Jainkoak bedeinka zaitzala," ta besteak "Ala biz," urkatzaille-esku auekin ikusi bai'niñuten. Aien beldurra adituz ezin esan nuan "Ala biz" erantzun, "Jainkoak bedeinka gaitzala esan zitenanean."

MACBETH ANDREA. Ez duk ortan ainbeste pentsatu bear.

MACBETH. Zergatik, ordea, "Ala biz" esan ezin nuan? Neu nintzan Jainkoaren esker bear aundienean zegona, ta "Ala biz" ito zan nire eztarrian.

MACBETH ANDREA. Zerak orrela artu ezkero, zoratu egingo giñake.

MACBETH. Mintzo bat entzun iduri zitzaidan oiuka ari zana "ez geiago lorik, Macbeth'ek loa il egin du!" Lo errugabea, arduraen matazatik ziriko aria iruten ari dana, loa egun bakoitzeko biziaren eriotza, lan nekatuaren bustialdia, gogo minduen gantzukaria, Izadi aundiaren bigarren maiekoa, bizitzaren oturuntzako janari aurrena . . .

MACBETH ANDREA. Zer esan nai duzu?

MACBETH. Ta otsak beti gelarik gela: "Ez geiago lorik!" Glamis'ek loa illarazi du ta au dala ta Cawdor'ek ez du lo geiago egingo, Macbeth'ek ez du lo geiago egingo!"

MACBETH ANDREA. Nor zan orrela oiu egiten zuna? Ene thane maite ori, ez argelerazi zure kemen zintzoa orrelakokeriak gogoan erabilliz. Zoaz ur billa lekuko zikin ori zure eskuetatik garbitzeko. Zergatik ekarri dituzu sastakai oriek

They must lie there: go carry them; and smear
The sleepy grooms with blood.

MACBETH. I'll go no more:
I am afraid to think what I have done;
Look on't again I dare not.

LADY MACBETH. Infirm of purpose!
Give me the daggers: the sleeping and the dead
Are but as pictures: 'tis the eye of childhood
That fears a painted devil. If he do bleed,
I'll gild the faces of the grooms withal;
For it must seem their guilt.

Exit. Knocking within

MACBETH. Whence is that knocking?
How is't with me, when every noise appals me?
What hands are here? ha! they pluck out mine eyes.
Will all great Neptune's ocean wash this blood
Clean from my hand? No, this my hand will rather
The multitudinous seas in incarnadine,
Making the green one red.

Re-enter LADY MACBETH

LADY MACBETH. My hands are of your colour; but I shame
To wear a heart so white.

Knocking within

I hear a knocking
At the south entry: retire we to our chamber;
A little water clears us of this deed:
How easy is it, then! Your constancy
Hath left you unattended.

Knocking within

Hark! more knocking.

gelatik? Antxe etzan bear dira. Zoaz eta
eramatzizu ta zikindu odolez gelazain lokartuak.

MACBETH. Ez naiz berriro joango;
egin dudanaz gogoeta egiteak ikaratzen nau.
Ez dut bekokirik ari berriz begiratzeko.

MACBETH ANDREA. Naimen aula!
Emazkidazu sastakaiak. Lo dagozanak eta illak itxura utsak besterik ez dira; deabruaren irudi baten aurrean dardar egiten dun aurraren begia da. Odola baldin ba'dario, gelazaiñen aurpegiak gorrituko ditut aren odolaren urreaz, erruak aiena irudi bear du ta.

Irtetzen da. Jotzen dute barruan

MACBETH. Nun jotzen dute?
Zer dut zarata txikienak izutzen naula?
Nolako eskuak dira oriek? A, begiok ateratzen dizkidate! Neptun'en itsaso aundi guziak ikuzi al lezake nire eskuen odol au? Ez, nire esku auek odol kolorea emango lioke itsaso ainbatu eziñari, urdinberdea gorri biurtuz!

MACBETH ANDREA sartzen da berriz

MACBETH ANDREA. Nire eskuok ere zureen koloretakoak dira: baiña lotsatuko nintzake biotz orren zuri bat eukitzeaz.

Jotzen dute

Egoaldeko atea jotzen dute.
Gure gelara gaitezen. Ur
tanta batek garbituko gaitu
egintza ontaz. Bai dala
erreza! Adorea galdu duzu

Jotzen dute

Entzun! Jotzen dute berriz ere. Jantzi zaitez gau-

Get on your nightgown, lest occasion call us,
And show us to be watchers. Be not lost
So poorly in your thoughts.

MACBETH. To know my deed, 'twere best not know myself.

Knocking within

Wake Duncan with thy knocking! I would thou couldst!

Exeunt

Scene 3

The same.

Knocking within. Enter a Porter

Porter. Here's a knocking indeed! If a
man were porter of hell-gate, he should have
old turning the key.

Knocking within

Knock,
knock, knock! Who's there, i' the name of
Beelzebub? Here's a farmer, that hanged
himself on the expectation of plenty: come in
time; have napkins enow about you; here
you'll sweat for't.

Knocking within

Knock,
knock! Who's there, in the other devil's
name? Faith, here's an equivocator, that could
swear in both the scales against either scale;
who committed treason enough for God's sake,
yet could not equivocate to heaven: O, come
in, equivocator.

soiñekoz, gerta bailiteke gure dei ta oeratu gabe egon gerala ageri egitea. Ez galdu zure burua orren iñulki zure gogoetan.

MACBETH. Nire egintza ezagun! Obe nuke nire burua ez ezagutzea!

Jotzen dute

Iratzarrazu Duncan zure jotzeaz! Ai ba'zeneza!

Irtetzen dira

3'garren agerraldia

Lengo lekua.

Ate jota barruan. Atezain bat sartzen da

ATEZAN. Au da jotzea esan bear dana! Gizon bat inpernuko atezain ba'litz izango luke giltzari bira bearra berandu arte.

Jotzen dute

Daun,
daun, daun! Nor da, Beltzebu'ren izenean? Uzta on baten itxaropena dagola ta urkatu dan landetxe-jaun bat al da? Zatoz mugonez. Ta ekarri zapi asko izerditu egin bearko duzu ta.

Jotzen dute

Daun,
daun! Nor da, beste deabruaren izenean? Ala fede! zimardika-gille bat da pisuaren edozein azpillaz zin egingo lukena beste azpillaren aurka; etoikeria egingo lukena Jainkoaren ederragatik, baiña bere zimardikak gora bera zerura ez zitekena. O, sar zaitez, ba, zimardikagille ori.

Knocking within

Knock,
knock, knock! Who's there? Faith, here's an
English tailor come hither, for stealing out of
a French hose: come in, tailor; here you may
roast your goose.

Knocking within

Knock,
knock; never at quiet! What are you? But
this place is too cold for hell. I'll devil-porter
it no further: I had thought to have let in
some of all professions that go the primrose
way to the everlasting bonfire.

Knocking within

Anon, anon! I pray you, remember the porter.

Opens the gate

Enter MACDUFF and LENNOX

MACDUFF. Was it so late, friend, ere you went to bed,
That you do lie so late?

Porter. Faith sir, we were carousing till the
second cock: and drink, sir, is a great
provoker of three things.

MACDUFF. What three things does drink especially provoke?

Porter. Marry, sir, nose-painting, sleep, and
urine. Lechery, sir, it provokes, and unprovokes;
it provokes the desire, but it takes
away the performance: therefore, much drink
may be said to be an equivocator with lechery:
it makes him, and it mars him; it sets
him on, and it takes him off; it persuades him,

Jotzen dute

Daun,
daun, daun! Nor da? Ala fede! Jostun ingeles bat da ori, galtzerdi prantzes batzu ostu ditula ta onara datorrena. Sar zaitez, jostuna. Emen berotu ditzakezu zure burdiñak.

Jotzen dute

Daun,
daun! Bein ere ez gelditu! Nor zaitut? Baiña leku au otzegia da inpernutzat. Ez dut gaurgero deabruaren atezain izan nai. Uste nuan udaberrizko bidean barna betiko su ontara doazan langintza guzietako lagunak sartzen utzi ditudala.

Jotzen dute

Berealaxe, berealaxe! Baiña ez aztu atezaiñaz.

Atea irikitzen du

MACDUFF eta LENNOX sartzen dira

MACDUFF. Ain berandu oeratu ziñan, adiskide, onen berandu jeikitzeko?

Atezain. Ala fede, jauna, jan-edaetan ari izan gera bigarren oillariterarte; ta edatea, jauna, iru gauzaren zirikatzaille aundia da.

MACDUFF. Zein iru gauza zirikatzen ditu bereziki edateak?

Atezain. Egundaiño, jauna: surgorritze, lozorro ta garnua. Lizunkeria berriz, zirikatu ta ibitu egiten du; naia zirikatzen du baiña burutzea gal-erazten. Orregatik esan diteke asko edatea zimardikagillea dala lizunkeriari buruz. Sortu ta deuseztu egiten du, ernarazi ta

and disheartens him; makes him stand to, and
not stand to; in conclusion, equivocates him
in a sleep, and, giving him the lie, leaves him.

MACDUFF. I believe drink gave thee the lie last night.

Porter. That it did, sir, i' the very throat on
me: but I requited him for his lie; and, I
think, being too strong for him, though he took
up my legs sometime, yet I made a shift to cast
him.

MACDUFF. Is thy master stirring?

Enter MACBETH

Our knocking has awaked him; here he comes.

LENNOX. Good morrow, noble sir.

MACBETH. Good morrow, both.

MACDUFF. Is the king stirring, worthy thane?

MACBETH. Not yet.

MACDUFF. He did command me to call timely on him:
I have almost slipp'd the hour.

MACBETH. I'll bring you to him.

MACDUFF. I know this is a joyful trouble to you;
But yet 'tis one.

MACBETH. The labour we delight in physics pain.
This is the door.

MACDUFF. I'll make so bold to call,
For 'tis my limited service.

elbarritu, eragin eta uzkurtu, zutitu ta zimurtu. Labur: amets batez zimardika egin eta gezurtatuz utzi egiten du.

MACDUFF. Uste dut edateak gezurra sartu dikala bart.

Atezain. Izan ere, jauna, zintzur-zintsurrean; baiña larrutik ordaindu dit bere gezurra, ta ura baiño indartsuagoa naizelakoan nago; aldi batean ankaetatik artu ba'nau ere, geroenean eskuratuko dut.

MACDUFF. Jeiki al duk ire ugazaba?

MACBETH sartzen da

Gure jotzeak iratzarri ditek; emen zetork.

LENNOX. Egun on, jaun zindo ori!

MACBETH. Egun on bioi.

MACDUFF. Errege jeiki al da, thane on ori?

MACBETH. Oraindik ez.

MACDUFF. Agindu zidan egundu baiño len ari dei egiteko ta beldur naiz ordua igaro ote dan.

MACBETH. Eramango zaitut arengana.

MACDUFF. Ba dakit gogozko nekea duzula au, baiña nekea gero ta gero ere.

MACBETH. Atsegin artzen dugun lanak bere nekea osatzen du. Au da atea.

MACDUFF. Sartuko naiz, zure baimenaz; eginbearra dut.

Exit MACDUFF

LENNOX. Goes the king hence to-day?

MACBETH. He does: he did appoint so.

LENNOX. The night has been unruly: where we lay,
Our chimneys were blown down; and, as they say,
Lamentings heard i' the air; strange screams of death,
And prophesying with accents terrible
Of dire combustion and confused events
New hatch'd to the woeful time: the obscure bird
Clamour'd the livelong night: some say, the earth
Was feverous and did shake.

MACBETH. 'Twas a rough night.

LENNOX. My young remembrance cannot parallel
A fellow to it.

Re-enter MACDUFF

MACDUFF. O horror, horror, horror! Tongue nor heart
Cannot conceive nor name thee!

MACBETH, LENNOX. What's the matter.

MACDUFF. Confusion now hath made his masterpiece!
Most sacrilegious murder hath broke ope
The Lord's anointed temple, and stole thence
The life o' the building!

MACBETH. What is 't you say? the life?

LENNOX. Mean you his majesty?

MACDUFF. Approach the chamber, and destroy your sight
With a new Gorgon: do not bid me speak;
See, and then speak yourselves.

Exeunt MACBETH and LENNOX

MACDUFF irtetzen da

LENNOX. Errege gaur al doa emendik?

MACBETH. Bai orrela erabaki du.

LENNOX. Gauza ikaragarria izan da. Etzan geran lekuan, aizeak gure kebideak lur-jo ditu, ta, diotenez auenak entzun dira aizean, eriotz garraisi bakanak; gizarte larrituarentzat sortu berriak diran istillu aundiak eta gertari nastuak mintzo izugarriz iragartzen zituten aotsak. Gautxoria gau osoan ari izan da urubika. Lurra dardaratu omen da sukarrez.

MACBETH. Gau latsa izan da.

LENNOX. Gazteegia naiz ala bezelako ezer gogoan izateko.

MACDUFF sartzen da berriz

MACDUFF. O, izugarri, izugarri, izugarri! Ez mingaiñak ea biotzak ezin dute zu iruditu ez izendatu.

MACBETH, LENNOX. Zer da, ba.

MACDUFF. Sarraskiak bere garako egintzak bururatu berria du! Eriotzegille dongeenak Jauna'k igurtziaren eliza itxustu ta bizia ostu du andik.

MACBETH. Zer diozu? Bizia?

LENNOX. Erregeari buruz mintzo al zera?

MACDUFF. Gelara urbil zaitezte ta itsu geldituko zerate Gorgona berriaren aurrean. Ez esan niri itz egin dezadala; Ikusazute ta gero itz egizute zerok!

MACBETH eta LENNOX irtetzen dira

Awake, awake!
Ring the alarum-bell. Murder and treason!
Banquo and Donalbain! Malcolm! awake!
Shake off this downy sleep, death's counterfeit,
And look on death itself! up, up, and see
The great doom's image! Malcolm! Banquo!
As from your graves rise up, and walk like sprites,
To countenance this horror! Ring the bell.

Bell rings

Enter LADY MACBETH

LADY MACBETH. What's the business,
That such a hideous trumpet calls to parley
The sleepers of the house? speak, speak!

MACDUFF. O gentle lady,
'Tis not for you to hear what I can speak:
The repetition, in a woman's ear,
Would murder as it fell.

Enter BANQUO

O Banquo, Banquo,
Our royal master 's murder'd!

LADY MACBETH. Woe, alas!
What, in our house?

BANQUO. Too cruel any where.
Dear Duff, I prithee, contradict thyself,
And say it is not so.

Re-enter MACBETH and LENNOX, with ROSS

MACBETH. Had I but died an hour before this chance,
I had lived a blessed time; for, from this instant,
There's nothing serious in mortality:
All is but toys: renown and grace is dead;

Esnatu, esnatu!
Jozute asalda-ezkilla! Sarraski ta etoikeri! Banquo ta Donalbain! Malcolm, esnatu! Astindu ezazute lo biguin ori, eriotzaren irudia, ta begirazute eriotza bera! Jeiki, jeiki ta ikuzazute Azken Epaiaren antza! Malcolm, Banquo! Jeiki zaitezte, zuen illobietatik bezela, ta ibilli iratxoen antzera laztura au begiztatzeko! Ezkilak jo.

Ezkillak jotzen du

MACBETH ANDREA sartzen da.

MACBETH ANDREA. Zer dala ta turuta ikaragarri orrek batzarrera dei egiten die etxe ontan lo datzatenei? Mintza, mintza!

MACDUFF. O, andre gozo ori.
Ez duzu on esan bear dizudana entzutea.
Emakume belarrik ezin lezake
jasan nire itzen birresatea.

BANQUO sartzen da.

O, Banquo, Banquo,
zure errege jauna sarraskitu dute.

MACBETH ANDREA. Ondikotz!
Ene, gurean!

BANQUO. Ankerregia nunnai!
Duff maite ori uka ezaiozu zure buruari,
arren, eta esaizu egia ez dala.

MACBETH eta LENNOX sartzen dira.

MACBETH. Ori gertatu baiño urtebete lenago baldin il banintz, aldi zoriontsu bat bizi izango nintzan; gaurgero, ordea, ez dago giza bizian balio danik; dana jostaillua da; aintza ta

The wine of life is drawn, and the mere lees
Is left this vault to brag of.

Enter MALCOLM and DONALBAIN

DONALBAIN. What is amiss?

MACBETH. You are, and do not know't:
The spring, the head, the fountain of your blood
Is stopp'd; the very source of it is stopp'd.

MACDUFF. Your royal father 's murder'd.

MALCOLM. O, by whom?

LENNOX. Those of his chamber, as it seem'd, had done 't:
Their hands and faces were an badged with blood;
So were their daggers, which unwiped we found
Upon their pillows:
They stared, and were distracted; no man's life
Was to be trusted with them.

MACBETH. O, yet I do repent me of my fury,
That I did kill them.

MACDUFF. Wherefore did you so?

MACBETH. Who can be wise, amazed, temperate and furious,
Loyal and neutral, in a moment? No man:
The expedition my violent love
Outrun the pauser, reason. Here lay Duncan,
His silver skin laced with his golden blood;
And his gash'd stabs look'd like a breach in nature
For ruin's wasteful entrance: there, the murderers,
Steep'd in the colours of their trade, their daggers
Unmannerly breech'd with gore: who could refrain,
That had a heart to love, and in that heart
Courage to make 's love known?

LADY MACBETH. Help me hence, ho!

aipua il dira. Biziaren ardoa isuri da ta
ondarrak besterik ez dira sotoan gelditu.

MALCOLM eta DONALBAIN sartzen dira.

DONALBAIN. Zer, ezbear bat?

MACBETH. Ura ez dakizuten
zuentzat. Zuen biziaren erroa, sorgua,
iturria aitu da; iturburua bera aitu da.

MACDUFF. Zure aita erregea sarraskitu dute.

MALCOLM. Ene, nork?

LENNOX. Aren gela zaiñek, dirudianez.
Aien eskuak eta aurpegia odolez xakiturik
zegozan eta alaber aien burkoen gaiñean
garbitu gabe arkitu genitun aien sastakaiak.
Begirada tinko, galdua zuten. Gizon bizi, bat
ere ez zan kalterik gabe egongo aien ondoan.

MACBETH. O, damu dut nire sumiñean
aiek il izateaz.

MACDUFF. Zergatik egin duzu?

MACBETH. Nor izan liteke zugur eta zozoa, neurridun
eta sumintsua, kirmen eta ezaxola bat-batera? Iñor ez.
Nire maitasun aserretuaren oldarra gogamen motelari
aurreratu zitzaion. Emen datza Duncan, bere
zillarrezko larrua urrezko odolez galartzutua, ta bere
zauri zabalak. izatezko atekak iduri, porrokaldi
ondatzaillearen sarbiderako. An, eriotzegilleak beren
langintzaren koloreaz zikinduta, beren sastakaiak odol
guriz zakarki jantzita. Nork, maitatzeko biotz bat eta
biotz ortan nola maitatzen dan erakusteko bear dan
adorea ba'du, nork geldierazi lezaioke bere buruari?

MACBETH ANDREA. Lagundu nazazute emendik irtetzeko!

MACDUFF. Look to the lady.

MALCOLM. [Aside to DONALBAIN] Why do we hold our tongues,
That most may claim this argument for ours?

DONALBAIN. [Aside to MALCOLM] What should be spoken here,
where our fate,
Hid in an auger-hole, may rush, and seize us?
Let 's away;
Our tears are not yet brew'd.

MALCOLM. [Aside to DONALBAIN] Nor our strong sorrow
Upon the foot of motion.

BANQUO. Look to the lady.

LADY MACBETH is carried out

And when we have our naked frailties hid,
That suffer in exposure, let us meet,
And question this most bloody piece of work,
To know it further. Fears and scruples shake us:
In the great hand of God I stand; and thence
Against the undivulged pretence I fight
Of treasonous malice.

MACDUFF. And so do I.

ALL. So all.

MACBETH. Let's briefly put on manly readiness,
And meet i' the hall together.

ALL. Well contented.

Exeunt all but MALCOLM and DONALBAIN.

MALCOLM. What will you do? Let's not consort with them:

MACDUFF. Izan ezazute andrearen ardura.

MALCOLM. [Berezian DONALBAIN'i] Zergatik isiltzen gera iñori
baiño geiago doakigun auzi ontan?

DONALBAIN. [MALCOLM'i berezian] Zer esan genezake emen
sarearte batean kukuturik dagon gure izangoa oldartu ta atzitu gaitzaken lekuan?
Iges dagigun.
Gure negarrak ez dira oraindik sortu.

MALCOLM. [DONALBAIN'i berezian] Ezta gure oiñaze biziak ezin dezake ere bere indar guziaz ekin.

BANQUO. Andrearen ardura izan ezazute.

MACBETH ANDREA eramaten dute

Ta otzetara jarrita ditugun gure larrugorriak estaldu
ditzagunean, bildu gaitezan eta azterkatu dezagun
odol-egintza au, obeki ezagutu dezaguntzat.
Beldurrak eta kezkak astintzen gaitute. Jainkoaren
esku altsuan dut uste-bidea, ta, bestalde, gertu nago
atoikeri gaizkindunaren asma isillakin
burrukatzeko.

MACDUFF. Ni ere bai!

GUZIAK. Baita guziak ere!

MACBETH. Berealakoan jantzi ta
elkargana gaitezan gizategian.

GUZIAK. Ongi deiskiogu.

MALCOLM eta DONALBAIN ez, beste guziak irtetzen dira.

MALCOLM. Zer diozu? Ez dezagun aiekin bat egin.

To show an unfelt sorrow is an office
Which the false man does easy. I'll to England.

DONALBAIN. To Ireland, I; our separated fortune
Shall keep us both the safer: where we are,
There's daggers in men's smiles: the near in blood,
The nearer bloody.

MALCOLM. This murderous shaft that's shot
Hath not yet lighted, and our safest way
Is to avoid the aim. Therefore, to horse;
And let us not be dainty of leave-taking,
But shift away: there's warrant in that theft
Which steals itself, when there's no mercy left.

Exeunt

Scene 4

Outside MACBETH's castle.

Enter ROSS and an Old Man

Old Man. Threescore and ten I can remember well:
Within the volume of which time I have seen
Hours dreadful and things strange; but this sore night
Hath trifled former knowings.

ROSS. Ah, good father,
Thou seest, the heavens, as troubled with man's act,
Threaten his bloody stage: by the clock, 'tis day,
And yet dark night strangles the travelling lamp:
Is't night's predominance, or the day's shame,
That darkness does the face of earth entomb,
When living light should kiss it?

Old Man. 'Tis unnatural,
Even like the deed that's done. On Tuesday last,
A falcon, towering in her pride of place,
Was by a mousing owl hawk'd at and kill'd.

Gizon xuriari errez zaio ez dun miña iduri egitea. Ingelanda'ra joango naiz.

DONALBAIN. Ta ni Irelanda'ra. Gure zoriak banadurik, ziurrago egongo gera. Emen ba dira sastakaiak parrez irrietan. Odolkideena odoltzaleena dugu.

MALCOLM. Eriotzegilleak egotzitako gezia aizean da oraiño, ta artezkarretik alde egitea dugu ziurrena. Zaldiz, beraz, ta ez dezagun kezkarik izan belearena egiten dugula ta. Zillegi baita lapur antzo iges egitea errukirik itxaron ez ditekenean.

Irtetzen dira

4'garren agerraldia

MACBETH'en gazteluaren aurrean.

ROSS eta Agure bat sartzen dira

Agure. Irurogei ta amar urte auetako gauzak ongi gogoratzen ditut.
Ordu ikaragarriak eta jazoera bakanak ikusita nago aietan; baiña gau lazkagarri onek uts bilakatzen du ezagutu dudan guzia.

ROSS. Ai, aitona,
ba dakusazu. Gizonaren egintzak nasturiko zeruak bere antzoki odoltsua zemaitzen du. Eguna da erlojuaren arauz ta, ori gora-gora, gau illunak argiontzi bidekaria estaltzen du. Gaua al da nagusi ala aguna lotsa da, argi biziak musu eman bear lioken lurraren aurpegia illuppeak estaltzen dulako?

Agure. Ori izadigaindikoa dugu, gertatu dana bezela. Lengo asteartean arro arro garaienera goititen zan aztore bat, saguak besterik jaten ez ditun untza batek il zun.

ROSS. And Duncan's horses—a thing most strange and cetain—
Beauteous and swift, the minions of their race,
Turn'd wild in nature, broke their stalls, flung out,
Contending 'gainst obedience, as they would make
War with mankind.

Old Man. 'Tis said they eat each other.

ROSS. They did so, to the amazement of mine eyes
That look'd upon't. Here comes the good Macduff.

Enter MACDUFF

How goes the world, sir, now?

MACDUFF. Why, see you not?

ROSS. Is't known who did this more than bloody deed?

MACDUFF. Those that Macbeth hath slain.

ROSS. Alas, the day!
What good could they pretend?

MACDUFF. They were suborn'd:
Malcolm and Donalbain, the king's two sons,
Are stol'n away and fled; which puts upon them
Suspicion of the deed.

ROSS. 'Gainst nature still!
Thriftless ambition, that wilt ravin up
Thine own life's means! Then 'tis most like
The sovereignty will fall upon Macbeth.

MACDUFF. He is already named, and gone to Scone
To be invested.

ROSS. Where is Duncan's body?

ROSS. Eta Duncan'en zaldiak—aundia baiña egia—ain eder eta ariñak, beren endaren kutunak, izaeraz aldaturik, beren ganbelak ausi ditute ostikoka ari dira ta ez dute men egin nai, gizadiaren aurka gudan bai'leuden.

Agure. Elkar jaten oi dute.

ROSS. Orixe egin dute, ikusi zuten nire begien arriduraren aurrean. Emen dator Macduff ona.

MACDUFF sartzen da.

Nola doa orain mundua, jauna?

MACDUFF. Zer, ez al dakusazu?

ROSS. Ezaguna al da egintza odoltsu baiño odoltsuago ori nork egin zun?

MACDUFF. Macbeth'ek il zitunak.

ROSS. Zorigaitzeko eguna!
Zer asmo ote zuten?

MACDUFF. Bustia artu zuten.
Malcolm eta Donalbain, erregearen bi
semeak gorputzari alde eragin eta itzuri
dira ta susmoa dago aien aurka.

ROSS. Izaearen aurka ori ere!
Zerorren biziaren giarrak irensten duzun aundinai ergel orrek!
Ortara ezkero, erregetza Macbeth'engana joango da, noski baiño noskiago.

MACDUFF. Izendatu dute dagoneko ta Scone'ra joan da nagusitza artzera.

ROSS. Nun dago Duncan'en gorputza?

MACDUFF. Carried to Colmekill,
The sacred storehouse of his predecessors,
And guardian of their bones.

ROSS. Will you to Scone?

MACDUFF. No, cousin, I'll to Fife.

ROSS. Well, I will thither.

MACDUFF. Well, may you see things well done there: adieu!
Lest our old robes sit easier than our new!

ROSS. Farewell, father.

Old Man. God's benison go with you; and with those
That would make good of bad, and friends of foes!

Exeunt

MACDUFF. Colme-kill'era eraman dute;
an daga aren asabaen illobi gurena ta bere
gorpuzkondoen gordelekua.

ROSS. Joango al zera Scone'ra?

MACDUFF. Ez, lengusu, Fife'ra noa.

ROSS. Ongi; joango naiz ara.

MACDUFF. Ederki, ikusiko al dituzu gauzak ongi andik. Agur.
Ta gure jantzi berriak zarrak baiño erarago datozkigula.

ROSS. Agur, aitona!

Agure. Jainkoaren onespena dioala zurekin eta gaitza on eta etsaiak
adiskide biurtu nai duten guziakin!

Irtetzen dira

Act 3

Scene 1

Forres. The palace. Enter BANQUO

BANQUO. Thou hast it now: king, Cawdor, Glamis, all,
As the weird women promised, and, I fear,
Thou play'dst most foully for't: yet it was said
It should not stand in thy posterity,
But that myself should be the root and father
Of many kings. If there come truth from them—
As upon thee, Macbeth, their speeches shine—
Why, by the verities on thee made good,
May they not be my oracles as well,
And set me up in hope? But hush! no more.

Sennet sounded. Enter MACBETH, as king, LADY MACBETH, as queen, LENNOX, ROSS, Lords, Ladies, and Attendants

MACBETH. Here's our chief guest.

LADY MACBETH. If he had been forgotten,
It had been as a gap in our great feast,
And all-thing unbecoming.

MACBETH. To-night we hold a solemn supper sir,
And I'll request your presence.

BANQUO. Let your highness
Command upon me; to the which my duties
Are with a most indissoluble tie
For ever knit.

MACBETH. Ride you this afternoon?

BANQUO. Ay, my good lord.

3'garren atala

1'go agerraldia

Forres'eko jauregia. Gizategi bat. BANQUO sartzen da

BANQUO. Guzia aiz onezkero: Errege, Cawdor, Glamis, guzia, emakume aztiak agindu bezela; baiña, joko zikiña egin ote dukan beldur nauk. Ala ere, aiek esan zitean nagusitza ez uala ire ondorekoetan geldituko ta nerau izango ninduala errege askoren erro ta aita. Aien aotik egia baldin irten ba'uan, iri esandakoaz erakusten dukanez, zergatik, irekiko egitiak izanik, ez lirake goi-erantzunak nirekiko izango, nire itxaropena goratuz? baiña ixo! aski da.

Turutotsa. MACBETH, errege jantsiz, MACBETH ANDREA, erregiña jantziz, LENNOX, ROSS, jaunak, andreak eta jarraigoa sartzen dira.

MACBETH. Emen dugu gure mai lagun nagusia.

MACBETH ANDREA. Artzaz aztu ba'giña uts bat izango genuke gure jai aundian, eta ez egokia, nolanai ere.

MACBETH. Apari aundi bat dugu gau ontan, jauna, ta artara dei egin dizugu.

BANQUO. Agindu ezazu, errege jauna; nire mentasuna zurekin elkartuta dago betiko lotura askatu eziñaz.

MACBETH. Zaldiz ibilliko zera arratsaldean?

BANQUO. Bai, jaun on ori.

MACBETH. We should have else desired your good advice,
Which still hath been both grave and prosperous,
In this day's council; but we'll take to-morrow.
Is't far you ride?

BANQUO. As far, my lord, as will fill up the time
'Twixt this and supper: go not my horse the better,
I must become a borrower of the night
For a dark hour or twain.

MACBETH. Fail not our feast.

BANQUO. My lord, I will not.

MACBETH. We hear, our bloody cousins are bestow'd
In England and in Ireland, not confessing
Their cruel parricide, filling their hearers
With strange invention: but of that to-morrow,
When therewithal we shall have cause of state
Craving us jointly. Hie you to horse: adieu,
Till you return at night. Goes Fleance with you?

BANQUO. Ay, my good lord: our time does call upon 's.

MACBETH. I wish your horses swift and sure of foot;
And so I do commend you to their backs. Farewell.

Exit BANQUO

Let every man be master of his time
Till seven at night: to make society
The sweeter welcome, we will keep ourself
Till supper-time alone: while then, God be with you!

Exeunt all but MACBETH, and an attendant

Sirrah, a word with you: attend those men
Our pleasure?

Attendant. They are, my lord, without the palace gate.

MACBETH. Gaurko batzarrean nai izango genun zure aolkua, beti zur eta onuratsua duguna, baiña biarko utziko dugu. Urrutira joango zera?

BANQUO. Bai, jauna, apal-ordurarte aldia emateraiñoko urrutira. Nire zaldia gibelkari ba'litz, ordu bat edo bi maillegatuko nizkioke gau illunari.

MACBETH. Ez uts egin gure jaiera.

BANQUO. Ez dut uts egingo, jauna.

MACBETH. Jakin dugu gure lengusu odolzaleak, bata Ingelanda'n eta bestea Irelanda'n dirala. Ez dute beren aita-erailtza aitortzen, baiña entzuleen belarriak ixtori bakanez betetzen ditute. Biar mintzatuko gera orretzaz eta guzioi dagozkigun beste Estadu-auzi batzuez. Ots, zaldiz! Agur, gabean itzuli zaitezen arte. Fleance al doa zurekin?

BANQUO. Bai, jaun on ori; aldiak ertsitzen gaitu.

MACBETH. Zaldi arin eta ziurrak opa dizkizuet eta aien ankaen gain jartzen zaituztet. Agur.

BANQUO irtetzen da

Bakoitza bere aldiaren jabe izan dedilla zazpirak arte. Bilgoa atsegiñago izan dakiguntzat soillik geldituko gera aparia arte. Ordurarte, Jainkoa zuekin.

MACBETH eta otsein bat ez, beste guziak irtetzen dira

Itz bat, lagun,
ordagoz oriek?

Otsein. Or dagoz, jauna, jauregiko ate ondoan.

MACBETH. Bring them before us.

Exit Attendant

To be thus is nothing;
But to be safely thus.—Our fears in Banquo
Stick deep; and in his royalty of nature
Reigns that which would be fear'd: 'tis much he dares;
And, to that dauntless temper of his mind,
He hath a wisdom that doth guide his valour
To act in safety. There is none but he
Whose being I do fear: and, under him,
My Genius is rebuked; as, it is said,
Mark Antony's was by Caesar. He chid the sisters
When first they put the name of king upon me,
And bade them speak to him: then prophet-like
They hail'd him father to a line of kings:
Upon my head they placed a fruitless crown,
And put a barren sceptre in my gripe,
Thence to be wrench'd with an unlineal hand,
No son of mine succeeding. If 't be so,
For Banquo's issue have I filed my mind;
For them the gracious Duncan have I murder'd;
Put rancours in the vessel of my peace
Only for them; and mine eternal jewel
Given to the common enemy of man,
To make them kings, the seed of Banquo kings!
Rather than so, come fate into the list.
And champion me to the utterance! Who's there!

Re-enter Attendant, with two Murderers

Now go to the door, and stay there till we call.

Exit Attendant

Was it not yesterday we spoke together?

First Murderer. It was, so please your highness.

MACBETH. Ekazkidazu onara.

Otsein irtetzen da

Onela izatea ez da ezer arrisku gabe baldin ez ba'naiz. Gure Banquo'rekiko beldurra barna da ta aren errege-itxuran ba-dakust zeren beldur izan. Oso oldarkoia da ta gogoaren olde ezikaitz orrekin ondore on egiteko kemena bidatzen dun zurtasuna elkartzen du. Ura kenduta, ez dago beldur diodanik. Eta nire gogoa malgutu egiten da berearen aurrean, Mark Andoni Kaisar'en aurrean malgutzen omen zan bezelaxe. Berak sorgiñak atarratu zitun, aurrenik errege izena eman zidatenean eta itz eragin zien. Ordun, iragarle antzo, errege lerro baten aitari bezela agur egin zioten. Koroia ez-ekarkorra jarri didate buruaren gaiñean, eta urrezigor elkorra eskuan, esku arrotz batek kenduko dizkidana, ez baitut ondorengorik. Baldin orrela ba'da, Banquo'ren jatorrikoentzat zikindu dut nire gogoa, aientzat illerazi dut Duncan onbera, aientzat bakarrik isuri dut gorrotoa nire bakearen edontzian, eta nire betiko bitxia gizon guztien arerioari eman diot aiek errege egiteko, Banquo'ren semeak errege egiteko! Ori baiño lenago, zatoz, Izango, gudatokira ta burruka dagigun il arte! Nor da?

Otseiña sartzen da berriz Eriotzegille bikin.

Oa ate ondora ta antxe egon nik dei egin arte.

Otseiña irtetzen da

Atzo itz egin genion elkarri, ezta?

Lenengo eriotzegille. Izan ere, atzo izan zan, zuri, jaun orri, on ba'zaizu.

MACBETH. Well then, now
Have you consider'd of my speeches? Know
That it was he in the times past which held you
So under fortune, which you thought had been
Our innocent self: this I made good to you
In our last conference, pass'd in probation with you,
How you were borne in hand, how cross'd, the instruments,
Who wrought with them, and all things else that might
To half a soul and to a notion crazed
Say 'Thus did Banquo.

First Murderer. You made it known to us.

MACBETH. I did so, and went further, which is now
Our point of second meeting. Do you find
Your patience so predominant in your nature
That you can let this go? Are you so gospell'd
To pray for this good man and for his issue,
Whose heavy hand hath bow'd you to the grave
And beggar'd yours for ever?

First Murderer. We are men, my liege.

MACBETH. Ay, in the catalogue ye go for men;
As hounds and greyhounds, mongrels, spaniels, curs,
Shoughs, water-rugs and demi-wolves, are clept
All by the name of dogs: the valued file
Distinguishes the swift, the slow, the subtle,
The housekeeper, the hunter, every one
According to the gift which bounteous nature
Hath in him closed; whereby he does receive
Particular addition from the bill
That writes them all alike: and so of men.
Now, if you have a station in the file,
Not i' the worst rank of manhood, say 't;
And I will put that business in your bosoms,
Whose execution takes your enemy off,
Grapples you to the heart and love of us,
Who wear our health but sickly in his life,
Which in his death were perfect.

MACBETH. Ederki. Nire itzak ausnartu al dituzute? Jakizute, ura izan zala ta ez, uste izan zenutenez, errugabe naizen au, beiñola zalaturik euki zinduztena. Gure lengo ikustaldian egietan eman nizuen ori. Erakutsi ere nizuen zearo, nola zilibokatu ta nola gaizki erabilli ziñuzten, nola jokatu zaituen, eta gogo-erdi bati, buru erotu bat ez danari: "Onatx Banquo'k egiña" esan erazi lezaioketen guziak.

Lenengo eriotzegille. Orixe ageri egin diguzu.

MACBETH. Egin dizuet, bai, ta areago egingo, ortarako baitugu gure bigarren ikustaldi au. Guzi ori eramateraiñoko egonarria al duzute? Orren berri on zaleak zerate ta gizon zintzo onen eta beronen aziaren alde otoi egingo al duzute, esku gogorrez, illobirantz bultzatu ta betiko teilla utsean bizi erazi zaituztelarik?

Lenengo eriotzegille. Gizonak gera, nagusi jauna.

MACBETH. Bai, lerrokadan gizontzat artuak zerate, xarlangoak, erbitxakurrak, endanastukoak, ur-txakurrak, artzaiñorak, epertxakurrak eta otso-txakurrak, guziek txakur izena duten bezelaxe; sari-lerroak, ordea. txaktur bizkorra, alperra, zolia, etxezaiña, eiztaria, bakoitza Izaera ongilleak eman dizkion tasunen arauz, eta ortatik artzen du deitura berezia, guziok erabat idatziak dagozan txartelan. Orobat gizonak. Beraz, baldin giza-lerroan azkenekoa ez dan lekua ba'duzute, esazute ta asma bat ageri egingo dizuet, baldin bururatzen ba'da, zuen etsai ezereztu ta gure biotz eta maitasarrearekin elkartu egiten zaituztena, sendotuko baituzute nire osasuna, galbidean ura bizi dan artean, eta ura il ezkero guzizkoa izango dana.

Second Murderer. I am one, my liege,
Whom the vile blows and buffets of the world
Have so incensed that I am reckless what
I do to spite the world.

First Murderer. And I another
So weary with disasters, tugg'd with fortune,
That I would set my lie on any chance,
To mend it, or be rid on't.

MACBETH. Both of you
Know Banquo was your enemy.

Both Murderers. True, my lord.

MACBETH. So is he mine; and in such bloody distance,
That every minute of his being thrusts
Against my near'st of life: and though I could
With barefaced power sweep him from my sight
And bid my will avouch it, yet I must not,
For certain friends that are both his and mine,
Whose loves I may not drop, but wail his fall
Who I myself struck down; and thence it is,
That I to your assistance do make love,
Masking the business from the common eye
For sundry weighty reasons.

Second Murderer. We shall, my lord,
Perform what you command us.

First Murderer. Though our lives—

MACBETH. Your spirits shine through you. Within this hour at most
I will advise you where to plant yourselves;
Acquaint you with the perfect spy o' the time,
The moment on't; for't must be done to-night,
And something from the palace; always thought
That I require a clearness: and with him—

Bigarren eriotzegille. Gizon bat nauzu, nagusi jauna, edozer egingo nukena munduaren aurka aspertzeko; onen sumindurik bainago aren ukaldi ta zartako zitalez.

Lenengo eriotzegille. Eta ni beste bat, nire bizia zirti-zarta jokatzeko gertu naizena, ura obetu ala galtaeko; ezbearrak onen nekatu ta zori txarrak onen gaizki erabillia nauzu ta.

MACBETH. Ba-dakizute biok:
Banquo izan dala zuen etsaia.

Bi Eriotzegilleak. Egia da, nire jauna.

MACBETH. Bai ta nirea ere, ta aren izatearen miñutu bakoitza nire biziaren biotzaren aurkako ukaldi bat izateraiñoko etsaigo odoltsu. Eta nire aginbidez, argi zabalean, nire begien aurretik ura ekortu ba'neza ere, nai dut esan eta beste gabe, ez dagokit ori egitea, aren adiskide batzuen ederragatik, nireak ere diranak aien maitasarrea ez baitut galdu nai, ta erasten dudanaren erorikoa deitoratu bear dut aien aurrean. Orregatik laguntza eske nagokizue guzien begietatik zera gordetzeko, arrazoi aundi batzu dirala ta.

Bigarren eriotzegille. Egingo dugu, nagusi, aginduko diguzun guzia.

Lenengo eriotzegille. Hai ta gure biziak—

MACBETH. Zure adorea argi agiri da. Ordu bete barru, goien-goienez, esango dizuet nun jarri bear zeraten, eta jakin eraziko dizuet egiteko une berezia. Gau ontan egin bear da ta jauregitik zertxobait aldera. Gogoratu ongi edozein susmotik aske gelditu bear dudala.

To leave no rubs nor botches in the work—
Fleance his son, that keeps him company,
Whose absence is no less material to me
Than is his father's, must embrace the fate
Of that dark hour. Resolve yourselves apart:
I'll come to you anon.

Both Murderers. We are resolved, my lord.

MACBETH. I'll call upon you straight: abide within.

Exeunt Murderers

It is concluded. Banquo, thy soul's flight,
If it find heaven, must find it out to-night.

Exeunt

Act 3, Scene 2

The palace.

Enter LADY MACBETH and a Servant

LADY MACBETH. Is Banquo gone from court?

Servant. Ay, madam, but returns again to-night.

LADY MACBETH. Say to the king, I would attend his leisure
For a few words.

Servant. Madam, I will.

Exit

LADY MACBETH. Nought's had, all's spent,
Where our desire is got without content:
'Tis safer to be that which we destroy
Than by destruction dwell in doubtful joy.

Enter MACBETH

Ta arekin batera lana uts eta akats gabea
izan dedin, laguntzen dun eta eriotza bere
aitarena bezain garrantzitsua zaidan Fleance
aren semeak, ordu illun onen alabearra ar
dezala. Erabakazute zerok berezian.
Bereala nator zuagana.

Bi Eriotzegilleak. Erabakia artu dugu, nire jauna.

MACBETH. Laster dei egingo dizuet. Geldi zaitezte barrenean.

Irtetzen dira

Au gertua da. Banquo, ire gogoak zerua arkitu bear
ba'du, gau ontan arkituko du.

Irtetzen da

3'garren atala. 2'garren agerraldia

Lengo lekua. Beste gizategi bat.

MACBETH ANDREA ta otsein bat sartzen dira.

MACBETH ANDREA. Banquo irten al da jauregitik?

Otseiña. Bai, ugazabandrea; baiñan itzuliko da gau ontan.

MACBETH ANDREA. Esaiok erregeari
itz batzu esan nai dizkiokala.

Otseiña. Ba-noa, ugazabandrea.

Otseiña ba-doa

MACBETH ANDREA. Ezer ez da irabazten eta guzia
galtzen, naia egin eta gogoa betetzen ez dugunean.
Obe da sarraskitu nai duguna izatea, sarraskitu ta
atsegin beldurtsu batean bizi izatea baiño.

MACBETH sartzen da

How now, my lord! why do you keep alone,
Of sorriest fancies your companions making,
Using those thoughts which should indeed have died
With them they think on? Things without all remedy
Should be without regard: what's done is done.

MACBETH. We have scotch'd the snake, not kill'd it:
She'll close and be herself, whilst our poor malice
Remains in danger of her former tooth.

But let the frame of things disjoint, both the worlds suffer,
Ere we will eat our meal in fear and sleep
In the affliction of these terrible dreams
That shake us nightly: better be with the dead,
Whom we, to gain our peace, have sent to peace,
Than on the torture of the mind to lie
In restless ecstasy. Duncan is in his grave;
After life's fitful fever he sleeps well;
Treason has done his worst: nor steel, nor poison,
Malice domestic, foreign levy, nothing,
Can touch him further.

LADY MACBETH. Come on;
Gentle my lord, sleek o'er your rugged looks;
Be bright and jovial among your guests to-night.

MACBETH. So shall I, love; and so, I pray, be you:
Let your remembrance apply to Banquo;
Present him eminence, both with eye and tongue:
Unsafe the while, that we
Must lave our honours in these flattering streams,
And make our faces vizards to our hearts,
Disguising what they are.

LADY MACBETH. You must leave this.

MACBETH. O, full of scorpions is my mind, dear wife!
Thou know'st that Banquo, and his Fleance, lives.

LADY MACBETH. But in them nature's copy's not eterne.

Zer duzu, jauna? Zergatik zaude bakarrik gogoeta goibelak zure lagun egiten dituzula? Ta sortu zitutenekin il bear izan zuten bulkoez estutua? Ongibiderik ez daukana aztu egin bear dugu. Egiña egin.

MACBETH. Sugeari ebaketa bat egin diogu, ez il, ordea. Osatu ta lengoa izango da berriz, eta bitartean gure gaiztokeri errukarria, aren ortzen arrisku pean dago.

Baiña, kolokatu bedi munduaren egitamua, zeru-lurrak irauzi bitez beldurrez jaten eta gabez dardarizatzen gaituten amets izugarri orien ersturan lo egiten jarraitzea baiño lenago. Obe dugu bakea irabaztearren bakera bidaldu genun zanarekin izatea, gogoa oiñaze eta eten gabeko larritasunean onela izatea baiño. Duncan bere illobian dago; biziaren sukarraldien ondoren, ongi lo egiten du. Etoikeria izan zun txarrena. Ez altzairuk, ez edenek, ez etxeko azpikeriek, ez arrotzen indarrek, ezerk ezin atzitu lezake.

MACBETH ANDREA. Ots, nire jaun gozo orrek, labaindu ezazu bekok zimurtu ori ager zaitez argi ta alai gaurko zure maikideen aurrean.

MACBETH. Orixe egingo dut, ene maite ori, ta egizu orobat zuk ere. Izan zaitez adeitsu Banquo'ri buruz. Obetsi ezazu begiz eta mingaiñez. Bai dala aldi arriskutsua gure omena zurikerizko uretan garbitu bear dugunean, bai ta ere aurpegiak gure biotzen zomorro egin aiek zer diran estaltzeko.

MACBETH ANDREA. Utzazu alde bat ori.

MACBETH. O, lugartsez josia dut gogoa, amazte maite ori! Ba-dakizu Banquo ta Fleance bizi dirala?

MACBETH ANDREA. Baiña es dira izadiaren betiko irudiak izango.

MACBETH. There's comfort yet; they are assailable;
Then be thou jocund: ere the bat hath flown
His cloister'd flight, ere to black Hecate's summons
The shard-borne beetle with his drowsy hums
Hath rung night's yawning peal, there shall be done
A deed of dreadful note.

LADY MACBETH. What's to be done?

MACBETH. Be innocent of the knowledge, dearest chuck,
Till thou applaud the deed. Come, seeling night,
Scarf up the tender eye of pitiful day;
And with thy bloody and invisible hand
Cancel and tear to pieces that great bond
Which keeps me pale! Light thickens; and the crow
Makes wing to the rooky wood:
Good things of day begin to droop and drowse;
While night's black agents to their preys do rouse.
Thou marvell'st at my words: but hold thee still;
Things bad begun make strong themselves by ill.
So, prithee, go with me.

Exeunt

Act 3, Scene 3

A park near the palace.

Enter three Murderers

First Murderer. But who did bid thee join with us?

Third Murderer. Macbeth.

Second Murderer. He needs not our mistrust, since he delivers
Our offices and what we have to do
To the direction just.

First Murderer. Then stand with us.
The west yet glimmers with some streaks of day:
Now spurs the lated traveller apace

MACBETH. Ortan dut itxarobide oraindik; kalte artu dezaketenak dira. Poztu zaitez, beraz. Saguzarrak bere egada estalia egaz egin baiño len; Hekate beltzaren deira, kakarraldoaren egal ezkatatsuak beren burruna lo-erazle gauaren ezkilla arrausi egillea jo dezaten baiño len, oroitza ikaragarrizko egintza bururatuko da emen.

MACBETH ANDREA. Zer da egiteko?

MACBETH. Geldi zaitez zure ezjakite errugabean,
uso maite-maitea, egiña txalotu arte . . . Zatoz, gau
itsutzaille ori, estali itzazu egun errukigarriaren
begi samurrak eta zure esku odoltsu ta ikus-eziñaz
urratu ta zatitu zurbillik naukan lotura aundi ori!
Argia iltzer dago ta belea abia daukan oianera
egaz doa. Egunaren izaki onak erortzen eta
lokartzen asi dira, gauaren egille beltzak beren
arrapakiñari oldaltzen zazkion artean. Nire itzok
arritzen zaitute. Ixo! Gaizki asitako gauzak
gaizkiaz sendotzen dira.
Zatoz, ba, zatoz nirekin.

Irtetzen dira

3'garren atala. 3'garren agerraldia

Zugazti bat jauregitik urbil.

Iru eriotzegille sartzen dira

Lenengo eriotzegille. Baiña, nork agindu dik gurekin etortzeko?

Irugarren eriotzegille. Macbeth'ek.

Bigarren eriotzegille. Ez dugu gibel beldurrik izan
bear, zeatz-zeatz beteko dugun eginbearra, esan
zigun ezkero.

Lenengo eriotzegille. Geldi zaitez, ba, gurekin.
Zenbait ozkorri ikusten dira oriandik Sartaldean.
Bidazti atseratuak bere zaldia aztalkatzen du,

To gain the timely inn; and near approaches
The subject of our watch.

Third Murderer. Hark! I hear horses.

BANQUO. [Within] Give us a light there, ho!

Second Murderer. 'Then tis he: the rest
That are within the note of expectation
Already are i' the court.

First Murderer. His horses go about.

Third Murderer. Almost a mile: but he does usually,
So all men do, from hence to the palace gate
Make it their walk.

Second Murderer. A light, a light!

Enter BANQUO, and FLEANCE with a torch

Third Murderer. 'Tis he.

First Murderer. Stand to't.

BANQUO. It will be rain to-night.

First Murderer. Let it come down.

They set upon BANQUO

BANQUO. O, treachery! Fly, good Fleance, fly, fly, fly!
Thou mayst revenge. O slave!

Dies. FLEANCE escapes

Third Murderer. Who did strike out the light?

First Murderer. Wast not the way?

Third Murderer. There's but one down; the son is fled.

mugonez ostaturatseko, ta igurikitzen duguna
urbil edo dabil.

Irugarren eriotzegille. Adizute! Zaldiak entzuten ditut.

BANQUO. [Barruan] Argi bat onara, oles!

Bigarren eriotzegille. Bera da,
nunbait. Gaiñerako maitarrak ba-
dira jauregi barruan.

Lenengo eriotzegille. Bere zaldiak itzuli egin dute.

Irugarren eriotzegille. Ia milla bateko bidean; baiñan
oitura da; beste guziak bezela, emendik jauregiko
ateraiño oiñez doaz.

Bigarren eriotzegille. Argi bat, argi bat!

BANQUO ta FLEANCE sartzen dira zuzi batekin

Irugarren eriotzegille. Bera da!

Lenengo eriotzegille. Zurt egon!

BANQUO. Euria izango da gau ontan.

Lenengo eriotzegille. Erori dedilla

BANQUO'ri oldartzen zazkio

BANQUO. O, salkeri! Iges egik, Fleance on orrek, iges, iges, iges!
I izango aut aspertzaille. O, etoi ori!

Iltzen da, FLEANCE'k iges egiten du

Irugarren eriotzegille. Nork itzali du argia?

Lenengo eriotzegille. Ez al zan bide onena?

Irugarren eriotzegille. Ez da erori bat baizik. Semeak iges egin du!

Second Murderer. We have lost
Best half of our affair.

First Murderer. Well, let's away, and say how much is done.

Exeunt

Scene 4

The same. Hall in the palace.

A banquet prepared. Enter MACBETH, LADY MACBETH, ROSS, LENNOX, Lords, and Attendants

MACBETH. You know your own degrees; sit down: at first
And last the hearty welcome.

Lords. Thanks to your majesty.

MACBETH. Ourself will mingle with society,
And play the humble host.
Our hostess keeps her state, but in best time
We will require her welcome.

LADY MACBETH. Pronounce it for me, sir, to all our friends;
For my heart speaks they are welcome.

First Murderer appears at the door

MACBETH. See, they encounter thee with their hearts' thanks.
Both sides are even: here I'll sit i' the midst:
Be large in mirth; anon we'll drink a measure
The table round.

Approaching the door

There's blood on thy face.

First Murderer. 'Tis Banquo's then.

MACBETH. 'Tis better thee without than he within.
Is he dispatch'd?

Bigarren eriotzegille. Gure egitekoaren erdi
oberena galdu dugu.

Lenengo eriotzegille. Ongi da; goazen eta eman dezagun egiñaren berri.

Irtetzen dira

4'garren agerraldia

Jauregiko gizategi nagusia. Oturuntza bat gerturik dago.

MACBETH, MACBETH andrea, ROSS, LENNOX, jaunak eta jarraigoa sartzen dira.

MACBETH. Ba-dakizkizute zeron maillak; eseri zaitezte.
Nire biotzeko ongi etorria guzioentzat.

Jaunak. Eskerrik asko, errege aundi ori.

MACBETH. Lagun artean nastuko gera,
maikide apal bat iduri. Gure ostatari andrea
beraren jarlekuan egongo da, baiña
mugonean ongi etorria eskatuko diogu.

MACBETH ANDREA. Emaiezu, jauna, niketz, gure adiskide guziai, ene biotzak ongi etorriak dirala dio ta.

Lenengo Eriotzegillea sartzen da ate ondoan gelditzen dala.

MACBETH. Ikusazu, aien biotzen eskarrak zugana
doaz. Bi aldeak ainbatekoak dira. Erdian eseriko naiz.
Poz zaitezte zuen gogara. Bereala zurrut bat artuko
dugu mai inguruka.

Atera urbiltzen da

Odola daukak aurpegian.

Lenengo eriotzegillea. Banquo'rena da, ba.

MACBETH. Ortara ezkero, obeki zegok ire gaiñean aren barnean baiño. Garbitu al duzute?

First Murderer. My lord, his throat is cut; that I did for him.

MACBETH. Thou art the best o' the cut-throats: yet he's good
That did the like for Fleance: if thou didst it,
Thou art the nonpareil.

First Murderer. Most royal sir,
Fleance is 'scaped.

MACBETH. Then comes my fit again: I had else been perfect,
Whole as the marble, founded as the rock,
As broad and general as the casing air:
But now I am cabin'd, cribb'd, confined, bound in
To saucy doubts and fears. But Banquo's safe?

First Murderer. Ay, my good lord: safe in a ditch he bides,
With twenty trenched gashes on his head;
The least a death to nature.

MACBETH. Thanks for that:
There the grown serpent lies; the worm that's fled
Hath nature that in time will venom breed,
No teeth for the present. Get thee gone: to-morrow
We'll hear, ourselves, again.

Exit Murderer

LADY MACBETH. My royal lord,
You do not give the cheer: the feast is sold
That is not often vouch'd, while 'tis a-making,
'Tis given with welcome: to feed were best at home;
From thence the sauce to meat is ceremony;
Meeting were bare without it.

MACBETH. Sweet remembrancer!
Now, good digestion wait on appetite,
And health on both!

LENNOX. May't please your highness sit.

Lenengo eriotzegillea. Lepo egin nion, jauna; neronek egin nion.

MACBETH. Lepo-egille onena aut; ala ere,
ona duk Fleance'rena moztu dukana. Baldin
i izan ba'aiz, berdin gabeko aut.

Lenengo eriotzegillea. Errege jauna,
Fleance'k iges egin zun.

MACBETH. Orrela ezkero, sukarraldia datorkit berriz. Narerik gelditukо nintzan, arrinabarra bezain trinkoa, arkaitza bezain sendoa, galerazpenik gabe, inguruko aizea bezain lokabea. Onela, ordea, nire burua zapatua burdiñetan eta beldur eta ezpai aogorriek uzkaldua dakust. Baiña Banquo segurean al dugu?

Lenengo eriotzegillea. Bai, jaun ona; segurean lubaki
baten zokondoan, buruan ogei aizto-ukaldi ditula,
aietako txikiena erioskoa edozeintzat.

MACBETH. Eskerrak orregatik.
Sugearenak egin du; itzuria dan
sugekumeak edena ekarriko du bere
aldian, baiña ez du ortzik oraiño. Zoaz,
biar itz egingo dugu elkarri berriz.

Eriotzegillea irtetzen da

MACBETH ANDREA. Ene errege jauna, ez duzu
poz-biderik ematen. Jaia nastu egiten da
eskeintzen dunak bere ongi etorria otsean-otsean
erakusten ez ba'die mai-lagunai. Bestela naiago
dugu gurean jatea. Bestalde, adiguria ongaillu
onena dugu ta edozein bilgo ura gabe utsa da.

MACBETH. Oroitarazle gozo ori!
Ots, egospen onak jangalea lagundu
dezala, ta osasuna bioi!

LENNOX. Eseri nai al duzu, errege aundi ori?

The GHOST OF BANQUO enters, and sits in MACBETH's place

MACBETH. Here had we now our country's honour roof'd,
Were the graced person of our Banquo present;
Who may I rather challenge for unkindness
Than pity for mischance!

ROSS. His absence, sir,
Lays blame upon his promise. Please't your highness
To grace us with your royal company.

MACBETH. The table's full.

LENNOX. Here is a place reserved, sir.

MACBETH. Where?

LENNOX. Here, my good lord. What is't that moves your highness?

MACBETH. Which of you have done this?

Lords. What, my good lord?

MACBETH. Thou canst not say I did it: never shake
Thy gory locks at me.

ROSS. Gentlemen, rise: his highness is not well.

LADY MACBETH. Sit, worthy friends: my lord is often thus,
And hath been from his youth: pray you, keep seat;
The fit is momentary; upon a thought
He will again be well: if much you note him,
You shall offend him and extend his passion:
Feed, and regard him not. [Aside to Macbeth]Are you a man?

MACBETH. Ay, and a bold one, that dare look on that
Which might appal the devil.

BANQUO'ren ITZALA sartzen da ta MACBETH'en lekuan eseritzen

MACBETH. Erriaren omen osoa genuke gure
tellatu pean Banquo gure lagun ederra emen
ba'lego. Naiago dut ari zabarkeria leporatzea,
zorigaitz bat dala ta ura deitoratzea baiño.

ROSS. Aren urrundeak, jauna, irain egiten
dio bere agintzari. On al zaizu, jaun aundi
ori, zure errege-laguntzarekin gu edertzea?

MACBETH. Mai guzia beterik dago.

LENNOX. Emen duzu leku berezi bat, jauna.

MACBETH. Nun?

LENNOX. Emen, jaun on ori. Zerk kezkarazten zaitu, errge
aundi ori?

MACBETH. Zuetako zeiñek egin du ori?

Jaunak. Zer, jauna?

MACBETH. Ezin esan dezakek ni izan naukala. Ez iñarrosi
nire aurka
ire adats odoldua.

ROSS. Jaunak, jeiki zaitezte, erregea ez dago ongi.

MACBETH ANDREA. Geldi zaitezte, adiskide onak.
Nire jaunak sarritan du ori gaztetandik. Eseri
zaitezte, arren. Kinka oldar batekoa da; Jesusean bere
baitaratzen da. Begira-begira baldin ba'zagozkio,
irain egingo diozute ta aren miña areagotuko.
Jazute ta ez egiozute so. [Berezian] Gizon ote zera?

MACBETH. Bai ta deabrua izutuko
lukenari so egiteraiñoko ausartua!

LADY MACBETH. O proper stuff!
This is the very painting of your fear:
This is the air-drawn dagger which, you said,
Led you to Duncan. O, these flaws and starts,
Impostors to true fear, would well become
A woman's story at a winter's fire,
Authorized by her grandam. Shame itself!
Why do you make such faces? When all's done,
You look but on a stool.

MACBETH. Prithee, see there! behold! look! lo! how say you?
Why, what care I? If thou canst nod, speak too.
If charnel-houses and our graves must send
Those that we bury back, our monuments
Shall be the maws of kites.

GHOST OF BANQUO vanishes

LADY MACBETH. What, quite unmann'd in folly?

MACBETH. If I stand here, I saw him.

LADY MACBETH. Fie, for shame!

MACBETH. Blood hath been shed ere now, i' the olden time,
Ere human statute purged the gentle weal;
Ay, and since too, murders have been perform'd
Too terrible for the ear: the times have been,
That, when the brains were out, the man would die,
And there an end; but now they rise again,
With twenty mortal murders on their crowns,
And push us from our stools: this is more strange
Than such a murder is.

LADY MACBETH. My worthy lord,
Your noble friends do lack you.

MACBETH. I do forget.
Do not muse at me, my most worthy friends,
I have a strange infirmity, which is nothing
To those that know me. Come, love and health to all;

MACBETH ANDREA. O, uskeria! Zure beldurrak egindako irudia duzu ori. Esan zenidanez Duncan'engana bidatzen ziñun aizezko sastakaia. O, orrako laztura ta dardar oriek-egizko beldurra irudikatzen dutenak-ederki letozke sutondoan, gizonaren baimenaz atso batek esaten dun ipuin batean. Au lotsa! Zer dala ta egiten dituzu orrelako keiñuak? Gero ta gero ere, aulki bateri baizik ez diozu begiratzen.

MACBETH. Ikusazu or, arren! Ots, begira!, so egizu! Zer diozu? Zer axola niri? Buruari eragin al ba'duzu, mintza zaitez ere. Ezurtegiek eta gure illobiek eortzi genitunak atzera bidaldu bear ba'dizkigute, saien sabelak izango ditugu eorztoki.

IRATXOA itzaltzen da

MACBETH ANDREA. Zer! Zoroarren gizontasuna galdu?

MACBETH. Ni emen ba'nago egon, nik ikusi dut!

MACBETH ANDREA. Ken ortik! Ori lotsa!

MACBETH. Odola isuri da orain baiño len, antziñean legeak gizartea garbitu ta eztitu baiño lenago. Eta geroago ere sarraskiak egin dira, ikaragarriegiak gure belarriendako. Lengo aldietetan, burmuiñak atera ezkero, gizona il egiten zan eta ura zan gizonaren azkena. Orain, ordea, buruan ogei eriozko sakailla ditutela birpiztu ta gure jarlekuetatik egozten gaitute. Eraitea bera baiño arrigarriagoa dugu au.

MACBETH ANDREA. Nire jaun zintzo ori, ba-dituzu zorrak zure adiskide martzalengana . . .

MACBETH. Aztu egin nuan.
Ez arritu nitzaz, ene adiskide jatorrak. Ba-dut eritasun bakan bat, ezer ez dana ezagutzen nautenentzat. Ots, osasun eta maitasun guziai.

Then I'll sit down. Give me some wine; fill full.
I drink to the general joy o' the whole table,
And to our dear friend Banquo, whom we miss;
Would he were here! to all, and him, we thirst,
And all to all.

Lords. Our duties, and the pledge.

Re-enter GHOST OF BANQUO

MACBETH. Avaunt! and quit my sight! let the earth hide thee!
Thy bones are marrowless, thy blood is cold;
Thou hast no speculation in those eyes
Which thou dost glare with!

LADY MACBETH. Think of this, good peers,
But as a thing of custom: 'tis no other;
Only it spoils the pleasure of the time.

MACBETH. What man dare, I dare:
Approach thou like the rugged Russian bear,
The arm'd rhinoceros, or the Hyrcan tiger;
Take any shape but that, and my firm nerves
Shall never tremble: or be alive again,
And dare me to the desert with thy sword;
If trembling I inhabit then, protest me
The baby of a girl. Hence, horrible shadow!
Unreal mockery, hence!

GHOST OF BANQUO vanishes

Why, so: being gone,
I am a man again. Pray you, sit still.

LADY MACBETH. You have displaced the mirth, broke the good meeting,
With most admired disorder.

MACBETH. Can such things be,
And overcome us like a summer's cloud,
Without our special wonder? You make me strange

Eseriko naiz. Emaidazute ardo, bete ezpain berdin. Topa maiean dauden guzien pozari ta emen ez dugun Banquo gure adiskide maiteari. Arren, etorriko al da! Zuei, ari! Topa guziai ta guzientzat.

Jaunak. Topa ta agur zuri.

IRATXOA sartzen da berriz

MACBETH. Atzera! Ken nire begitik! Lurrak estalduko al au! Ire ezurrek ez ditek muiñik, ire odola otza duk. Ez zegok ikusmenik su egozten diteken begioetan!

MACBETH ANDREA. Ez ikusi ortan, adiskide onak, oiturazko gauza bat baizik; ez da besterik. Ondatzen du, ordea, garaiaren atsegiña.

MACBETH. Ausartzen nauk gizon bat ausartzen dukan edozertara. Urbil adi Errusi'ko artz illetsu baten, adar bakar izkilludun naiz Hirkani'ko katamotzaren antzean. Ori ez, edozein karantza ar zak eta nire kirio sendoak ez ditek ikararik egingo, ala bizi adi berriz eta aupada egidak eremuan ezpataz, eta ordun etxean dardarka gelditzen ba'nauk aldarrika nazak neskato baten andrakilla. Utikan, itzal izugarri ori!

IRATXOA itzaltzen da

Ongi, orrela, ura joan ezkero gizona nauk berriz. Eseri zaitez, mesedez.

MACBETH ANDREA. Poza oildu duzu, zorakeri arrigarrienaz ba'tzaldi gozatsua ausiz.

MACBETH. Gertatu al ditekez orrelako zerak eta gure buruen gaiñean erori uda odei bat iduri, txundioak gu artu gabe? Neronen

Even to the disposition that I owe,
When now I think you can behold such sights,
And keep the natural ruby of your cheeks,
When mine is blanched with fear.

ROSS. What sights, my lord?

LADY MACBETH. I pray you, speak not; he grows worse and worse;
Question enrages him. At once, good night:
Stand not upon the order of your going,
But go at once.

LENNOX. Good night; and better health
Attend his majesty!

LADY MACBETH. A kind good night to all!

Exeunt all but MACBETH and LADY MACBETH

MACBETH. It will have blood; they say, blood will have blood:
Stones have been known to move and trees to speak;
Augurs and understood relations have
By magot-pies and choughs and rooks brought forth
The secret'st man of blood. What is the night?

LADY MACBETH. Almost at odds with morning, which is which.

MACBETH. How say'st thou, that Macduff denies his person
At our great bidding?

LADY MACBETH. Did you send to him, sir?

MACBETH. I hear it by the way; but I will send:
There's not a one of them but in his house
I keep a servant fee'd. I will to-morrow,
And betimes I will, to the weird sisters:
More shall they speak; for now I am bent to know,
By the worst means, the worst. For mine own good,
All causes shall give way: I am in blood
Stepp'd in so far that, should I wade no more,

kemenaz zalantzan jartzen nauzu, orrelako ikuskariak begiztatu ta zure masailletako sortzezko gorri garbia gorde dezakezula, nireak beldurrarren zuritzen diran artean.

ROSS. Zeintzu ikuskari, jauna?

MACBETH ANDREA. Ez mintzatu, arren. Geroago ta gaizkiago doa. Edozein galdek sumintzen du. Beraz, gabon! Ez axolatu zoazten era dala ta; zoazte bereala.

LENNOX. Gau on eta osasun obea, errege jauna.

MACBETH ANDREA. Gau on guzioi!

Jaunak eta jarraigoa irtetzen dira

MACBETH. Bai, odola nai du! Odola odol eske, esan oi da. Arriak igitzen eta zugatzek mintzatzen ikusi dira. Ta aztiantzek eta zerarekin elikartuak agertzen ziran gertariek. bela, belatxinga ta mikaen mintzoz eraille ezkutatuena salatu dute . . . Nola doa gaua?

MACBETH ANDREA. Goizarekin burrukan norgeiagoka.

MACBETH. Zer uste duzu gure dei agiria astantzen dun Macduff'ez?

MACBETH ANDREA. Etortzeto agiadu al zenion, jauna?

MACBETH. Alabearrean dakit; baita norbait igorriko diot. Ba-daukat nit bustiriko otsein bat aren etxe guzietan. Biar—eta goizean goiz—Aizpa Aztiak ikustera joango naiz. Ta areago esango didate, jakin bear baitut txarrena bide txarrenez. Danak amor egingo du nire onaren aurrean. Odol ibaiean ain urrutira joan naiz eta aurreratzenago ez

Returning were as tedious as go o'er:
Strange things I have in head, that will to hand;
Which must be acted ere they may be scann'd.

LADY MACBETH. You lack the season of all natures, sleep.

MACBETH. Come, we'll to sleep. My strange and self-abuse
Is the initiate fear that wants hard use:
We are yet but young in deed.

Exeunt

Scene 5

A Heath. Thunder. Enter the three Witches meeting HECATE

First Witch. Why, how now, Hecate! you look angerly.

HECATE. Have I not reason, beldams as you are,
Saucy and overbold? How did you dare
To trade and traffic with Macbeth
In riddles and affairs of death;
And I, the mistress of your charms,
The close contriver of all harms,
Was never call'd to bear my part,
Or show the glory of our art?
And, which is worse, all you have done
Hath been but for a wayward son,
Spiteful and wrathful, who, as others do,
Loves for his own ends, not for you.
But make amends now: get you gone,
And at the pit of Acheron
Meet me i' the morning: thither he
Will come to know his destiny:
Your vessels and your spells provide,
Your charms and every thing beside.
I am for the air; this night I'll spend
Unto a dismal and a fatal end:
Great business must be wrought ere noon:
Upon the corner of the moon
There hangs a vaporous drop profound;

joatekotan atzeratzea araindiratzea bezain
gaitza izango da. Ausnartu baiño len eskuak
bete bear ditun gauza berriak ditut buruan.

MACBETH ANDREA. Edozein sorkari ontsen duna bear duzu: lo.

MACBETH. Zatoz, goazen lotara. Nire zorapen bakan au oitura
gogor baten bearra dun beldur asiberri bat da.
Ikasleak gera oraindik egintzan.

Irtetzen dira

5'garren agerraldia

Gain batean. Ekaitza. HEKATE sartu ta iru sorgiñak arkitzen ditu.

Lenengo Sorgiña. Zer duzu, Hekate? Aserre dirudizu.

HEKATE. Ez al dut aserretzeko biderik,
atso aogorri, sarkoi orret? Nola izan
duzute bekoki Macbeth'ekin salerosten
eta ar ematen ari izateko papaita ta
eriotz gaietan, eta niri, zuen lilluraen
jabe, gaitz guzien asmatzaille isil oni ez
didazute bein-ez-bein dei egin
eskuartzeko edo gure antzearen aintza
erakusteko? Ta auxe da txarrena: egin
duzuten guzia seme aldartetsu, aidur
eta suminkor baten alde izan da,
besteak bezela, ez zaituena maite zeron
ederragatik beraren xedeengatik baizik.
Ongitu itzazute, beraz, zuen okerrak,
bazter zaitezte ta iguriki nazazute biar
Akeronte'ko lezean, ara etorriko baita
bera bere izangoa ezagutzeko. Gertu
itzazute zuen ontzi, lillurakeri,
sorginkeri ta gaiñerako guziakin.
Aizeetara igoko naiz ta asmo gaizto
baten betetzean emango dut gau au.
Gaberdia gabe gertari aundi bat
zertuko da. Lurrun tanta luze bat

I'll catch it ere it come to ground:
And that distill'd by magic sleights
Shall raise such artificial sprites
As by the strength of their illusion
Shall draw him on to his confusion:
He shall spurn fate, scorn death, and bear
He hopes 'bove wisdom, grace and fear:
And you all know, security
Is mortals' chiefest enemy.

Music and a song within: "Come away, come away," & c.

Hark! I am call'd; my little spirit, see,
Sits in a foggy cloud, and stays for me.

Exit

First Witch. Come, let's make haste; she'll soon be back again.

Exeunt

Scene 6

Forres. The palace.

Enter LENNOX and another Lord

LENNOX. My former speeches have but hit your thoughts,
Which can interpret further: only, I say,
Things have been strangely borne. The
gracious Duncan
Was pitied of Macbeth: marry, he was dead:
And the right-valiant Banquo walk'd too late;
Whom, you may say, if't please you, Fleance kill'd,
For Fleance fled: men must not walk too late.
Who cannot want the thought how monstrous
It was for Malcolm and for Donalbain
To kill their gracious father? damned fact!
How it did grieve Macbeth! did he not straight

zintzilika dago illargiaren adarretik.
Lurrera baiño len artuko dut eta azti-
arteziz ura iragaziz, ura galkuntzara
eramango duten gaiztozkoak sortu
eraziko ditut artatik.
Alaberra gutxietsiko du, eriotza isekatuko ta
jakintza, erruki ta beldurraren gaiñetik
eramango ditu bere itxaropenak. Eta zuek ba-
dakizute ustekaria dute ilkorrek etsai aundiena.

Kantu bat barruan

Zatoz onara, zatoz onara, ta abar. Adizute! Dei egiten didate.
Ikusazute: nire iratxo txikia odei laiñotsu batean eseri ta nire begira dago.

Irtetzen da

Lenengo Sorgiña. Zatozte, laster egin dezagun. Berealakoan etorriko da berriz.

Irtetzen da

6'garren agerraldia

Forres. Jauregiko gizategi bat.

LENNOX eta beste jaun bat sartzen dira.

LENNOX. Nire lengo itzek zure gogoetak, jo baizik ez dute egin; zure gain aiek adi-eraztea. Bakarrik esango dut gauzak oi-ez bezela bururatu dirala. Macbeth'ek Duncan zindoa deitoratu du; egundaiño, illa zan! Eta Banquo kementsua beranduegi egurastu zan . . . Esan dezakezu, on ba'zaizu, Fleance'k il zula, Fleance'k iges egin du ta; ez da on beranduegi egurasturik artzea. Nork ez ote du oldoztuko Malcolm eta Donalbain'ek beren aita bikaiña il-eraztean, izaera aurkako egintza bat zertu zutela! Ori gaizki nardagarria! Zenbateraiño

In pious rage the two delinquents tear,
That were the slaves of drink and thralls of sleep?
Was not that nobly done? Ay, and wisely too;
For 'twould have anger'd any heart alive
To hear the men deny't. So that, I say,
He has borne all things well: and I do think
That had he Duncan's sons under his key—
As, an't please heaven, he shall not—they
should find
What 'twere to kill a father; so should Fleance.
But, peace! for from broad words and 'cause he fail'd
His presence at the tyrant's feast, I hear
Macduff lives in disgrace: sir, can you tell
Where he bestows himself?

LORD. The son of Duncan,
From whom this tyrant holds the due of birth
Lives in the English court, and is received
Of the most pious Edward with such grace
That the malevolence of fortune nothing
Takes from his high respect: thither Macduff
Is gone to pray the holy king, upon his aid
To wake Northumberland and warlike Siward:
That, by the help of these—with Him above
To ratify the work—we may again
Give to our tables meat, sleep to our nights,
Free from our feasts and banquets bloody knives,
Do faithful homage and receive free honours:
All which we pine for now: and this report
Hath so exasperate the king that he
Prepares for some attempt of war.

LENNOX. Sent he to Macduff?

LORD. He did: and with an absolute "Sir, not I,"
The cloudy messenger turns me his back,
And hums, as who should say "You'll rue the time
That clogs me with this answer."

LENNOX. And that well might
Advise him to a caution, to hold what distance

atsegabetu zun Macbeth! Edariaren jopu ta loaren menpekoak ziran bi errudunak ez al zitun berberean sarraskitu bere aserre doneen? Ez al zan ontan zindoki ari izan? Bai ta zugurki ere; gizon aiek egiña ukatzen entzuteak edozein biotza suminduko baitzun. Labur: gauza guziak ongi eraman ditula diot, eta uste ere dut, Duncan'en semeak giltzapean ba'leduzka—Jainkoak ori ez detsala!—aita bat il-eraztea zer dan jakingo luketela; ta Fleance'k alaber. Baiñan, ixo! Entzunik bainago Macduff'ek zabalki mintzatzeagatik eta tiranuaren jaia uts egiteagatik aren ederra galdu dula. Jauna, esan al dezaidazuke nun gerizatzen dan?

JAUNA. Tiranu onek, jaiotzez zor zaiona kendu dion Duncan'en semea, Ingelanda'ko errege-irian bizi da. Edorta'k guziz jainkotiarrak txera ain ona egin dio ta zoriaren gaizkinaiak ez du zor zaion lotsa aundiaz gabetu. Ara joana duzu Macduff, Siward gudakaria ta bere Northumberlandarrek laguntza eman dezaiotela eskatzera, errege gurenari, aien urgaizgoaren bidez—ta egintza indartuko dun Goikoa'ri esker—berriz euki al dezagun janaria gure maietan, loa gure gauetan ta gure jai ta orritsetatik sastakai odoltsuak kendu, zuzenbidezko ziñak egin eta aginbideak lasaiki artu; ots, gaur egunean irrikitzen ditugun gauza guztiok. Eta berri orrek erregea errenbesteraiño aserre-erazi du ta gudarako gertutzen ari da.

LENNOX. Ta igerri al du iñor Macduff'en billa?

JAUNA. Bai, ta "Ez, jauna" biribil bat entzunik, mandatari beltzak atzea eman zun marmarka esan bai'lun: "Damu izango duzu erantzun onek oztopo emango didan aldiaz."

LENNOX. Gaztigu ori on izango du zurt egoteko ta bere zugurtzak aolkatuko dion

His wisdom can provide. Some holy angel
Fly to the court of England and unfold
His message ere he come, that a swift blessing
May soon return to this our suffering country
Under a hand accursed!

Lord. I'll send my prayers with him.

Exeunt

urruntasunean burua gordetzeko. Aingeru santuren batek landa'ko errege-irira egaz egin eta bere gezna azalduko al du, ura ara baiño len, esku madarikatu baten pean dagon gure erri ontara bedeinkapen laster bat etorri dedin.

JAUNA. Nire otoiak lagun dakizkiola.

Irtetzen dira

Act 4

Scene 1

A cavern. In the middle, a boiling cauldron.

Thunder. Enter the three Witches

First Witch. Thrice the brinded cat hath mew'd.

Second Witch. Thrice and once the hedge-pig whined.

Third Witch. Harpier cries 'Tis time, 'tis time.

First Witch. Round about the cauldron go;
In the poison'd entrails throw.
Toad, that under cold stone
Days and nights has thirty-one
Swelter'd venom sleeping got,
Boil thou first i' the charmed pot.

ALL. Double, double toil and trouble;
Fire burn, and cauldron bubble.

Second Witch. Fillet of a fenny snake,
In the cauldron boil and bake;
Eye of newt and toe of frog,
Wool of bat and tongue of dog,
Adder's fork and blind-worm's sting,
Lizard's leg and owlet's wing,
For a charm of powerful trouble,
Like a hell-broth boil and bubble.

ALL. Double, double toil and trouble;
Fire burn and cauldron bubble.

Third Witch. Scale of dragon, tooth of wolf,
Witches' mummy, maw and gulf
Of the ravin'd salt-sea shark,
Root of hemlock digg'd i' the dark,

4'garren atala

1'go agerraldia

Arpe illun bat. Erdia, pertz bat galgalka.

Ostotsak. Iru sorgiñak sartzen dira

Lenengo Sorgiña. Irutan katu nabarra miauka.

Bigarren Sorgiña. Irutan eta bein trikuak ulu.

Irugarren Sorgiña. Atxoak ots dagi: "Ordu da, ordu!"

Lenengo Sorgiña. Pertzaren ingurun ibil gaitezan
ta errai zitalduak ditzagun bota an.
Arri otz azpian ogei ta hamaika
egunez ta gauez lotan, pozoiña
izerditu duzun lugartza zu izan
zaitez lenengoa sorgindu saldan.

GUZIAK. Nekeak ta kezkak berretzen ekin;
suak erre beza, pertzak irakin.

Bigarren Sorgiña. Zingiraetako auge-azpizunki
pertzera jaurtikita an egos bedi.
Surangil-begia, ta igel-beatzak,
saguzar-illeak, txakur mingaiñak,
sugegorri-ortzak, lugartz-eztenak,
mirotz-atzaparrak, gabontz-egoak;
Sorgin-lillura altsu bat egiteko,
birakite, inpernu salda bat antzo.

GUZIAK. Nekeak ta kezkak berretzen ekin;
suak erre beza, pertzak irakin.

Irugarren Sorgiña. Irantsuge-ezkatak eta otso-agiñak,
sorgin-gorputzillaz egindako autsak,
marrazo zintzurkoi baten urdailla,
illuntan idoki otzeibelarra,

Liver of blaspheming Jew,
Gall of goat, and slips of yew
Silver'd in the moon's eclipse,
Nose of Turk and Tartar's lips,
Finger of birth-strangled babe
Ditch-deliver'd by a drab,
Make the gruel thick and slab:
Add thereto a tiger's chaudron,
For the ingredients of our cauldron.

ALL. Double, double toil and trouble;
Fire burn and cauldron bubble.

Second Witch. Cool it with a baboon's blood,
Then the charm is firm and good.

Enter HECATE to the other three Witches

HECATE. O well done! I commend your pains;
And every one shall share i' the gains;
And now about the cauldron sing,
Live elves and fairies in a ring,
Enchanting all that you put in.

Music and a song: "Black spirits," & c.

HECATE retires

Second Witch. By the pricking of my thumbs,
Something wicked this way comes.
Open, locks,
Whoever knocks!

Enter MACBETH

MACBETH. How now, you secret, black, and midnight hags!
What is't you do?

ALL. A deed without a name.

Judu birao-ontzi baten gibela,
aker-beazuna ta izai-adarrak.
illargi gabeko gaban moztuak;
Tartar-ezpaiñak ta turko-sudurra,
jaiotzean ito ta ama gaiztoak
obira bota-ume baten beatzak;
egizute orea ligatsu, lodi;
katamotz-erraiak orain ezarri,
beste guziakin ditezan nasi.

GUZIAK. Nekeak ta kezkak berretzen ekin;
suak erre beza, pertzak irakin.

Bigarren Sorgiña. Tximuren odolaz oztu guzia
ta gertu dagoke sorgin lillura

HEKATE sartzen da

HEKATE. Ederki! Goresten dut zuen lana,
bakoitzak ba-duke saria ainbana.
Eta orain guziek lapiko ingurun,
mamuem antzera, kanta dagigun,
ta gure kantuaz, artan ezarri
duzuten guzia sorgindu bedi.

Soiñua ta abestia: "Gogo beltzak"

HEKATE irtetzen da

Bigarren Sorgiña. Beatzen aznaiak iragartzen dit
madarikatu bat urbiltzen dala.
Morroillo oriek, zaitezte iriki
ateak norknai jotzen ditula!

MACBETH sartzen da

MACBETH. Zertan ari al zerate, zuek gau-erdiko sorgin beltz, ezkutuok?

GUZIAK. Izenik gabeko lan batetan.

MACBETH. I conjure you, by that which you profess,
Howe'er you come to know it, answer me:
Though you untie the winds and let them fight
Against the churches; though the yesty waves
Confound and swallow navigation up;
Though bladed corn be lodged and trees blown down;
Though castles topple on their warders' heads;
Though palaces and pyramids do slope
Their heads to their foundations; though the treasure
Of nature's germens tumble all together,
Even till destruction sicken; answer me
To what I ask you.

First Witch. Speak.

Second Witch. Demand.

Third Witch. We'll answer.

First Witch. Say, if thou'dst rather hear it from our mouths,
Or from our masters?

MACBETH. Call 'em; let me see 'em.

First Witch. Pour in sow's blood, that hath eaten
Her nine farrow; grease that's sweaten
From the murderer's gibbet throw
Into the flame.

ALL. Come, high or low;
Thyself and office deftly show!

Thunder. First Apparition: an armed Head

MACBETH. Tell me, thou unknown power,—

First Witch. He knows thy thought:
Hear his speech, but say thou nought.

First Apparition. Macbeth! Macbeth! Macbeth! beware Macduff;
Beware the thane of Fife. Dismiss me. Enough.

MACBETH. Nolanai zuengandu duzuten, jakintza orren izenean, arren eta arren eskatzen dizuet niri erantzuteko. Aizeak askatu ta elizaen aurka oldartu eragin bear ba'diezute ere; nai ta uin apartuak ontziak nastu ta irentsi, nai ta ernemiñean dagon garia zimeldu ta zugatzak lurreratu; nai ta gazteluak beren jabeen gaiñera erroiztu; nai ta jauregiak eta piramideak bere gaiña oiñarriarekin elkartu; nai ta izadiaren azien altxorra osotara irauli, ausiabartza bera ere nekarazi arte, erantzuidazute!

Lenengo Sorgiña. Mintza.

Bigarren Sorgiña. Galde.

Irugarren Sorgiña. Guk erantzungo.

Lenengo Sorgiña. Esan, naiago duk gure aotik entzun ala gure nagusiengandik?

MACBETH. Dei egiezute, ikus ditzadan!

Lenengo Sorgiña. Bere bederatzi zerri-ordotxak irentsi ditun urdamaren odola urkatu baten sokaren koipeaz nastu ta bota dezagun guzia sutara.

GUZIAK. Ator, gogo gaizto, aundi naiz txiki,
ta ire eginbearra egik egoki.

Ostotsak. Babesez estalitako buru bat agertzen da

MACBETH. Esaidak, almen ez-ezagun orrek—

Lenengo Sorgiña. Ba-zekik ire gogamena.
Adi zak eta isilik ago.

Agerpena. Macbeth, Macbeth, Macbeth! Kontu Macduff'ekin! Kontu Fife'ko thanearekin! Utzi nazazute! Aski da.

Descends

MACBETH. Whate'er thou art, for thy good caution, thanks;
Thou hast harp'd my fear aright: but one
word more,—

First Witch. He will not be commanded: here's another,
More potent than the first.

Thunder. Second Apparition: A bloody Child

Second Apparition. Macbeth! Macbeth! Macbeth!

MACBETH. Had I three ears, I'd hear thee.

Second Apparition. Be bloody, bold, and resolute; laugh to scorn
The power of man, for none of woman born
Shall harm Macbeth.

Descends

MACBETH. Then live, Macduff: what need I fear of thee?
But yet I'll make assurance double sure,
And take a bond of fate: thou shalt not live;
That I may tell pale-hearted fear it lies,
And sleep in spite of thunder.

Thunder. Third Apparition: a Child crowned, with a tree in his hand

What is this
That rises like the issue of a king,
And wears upon his baby-brow the round
And top of sovereignty?

ALL. Listen, but speak not to't.

Third Apparition. Be lion-mettled, proud; and take no care
Who chafes, who frets, or where conspirers are:
Macbeth shall never vanquish'd be until
Great Birnam wood to high Dunsinane hill
Shall come against him.

Beratzen da

MACBETH. Aizena aizela, eskerrik asko ire aolku onarengatik. Nire beldurra igarri duk. Baiña itz bat geiago,—

Lenengo Sorgiña. Ez dik agindurik artzen; emen duk lenbizikoa baiño altsuago bat.

Ostotsak. Aur odoldu bat agertzen da

Bigarren Agerpena. Macbeth, Macbeth, Macbeth!

MACBETH. Iru belarri ba'nuzka irurekin adituko nizueke.

Bigarren Agerpena. Izan adi odolkoi, kementsu ta oldarkoia. Irri egiok gizonaren al izateari, emakumegandik jayo bat ere ezin baitezaioke Macbeth'i kalte egin.

Beratzen da

MACBETH. Ortara ezkero, bizi adi, Macduff! Zergatik naiteke ire beldur? Baiña segurantza seguragoa egingo dut eta alabearraren aurka sendotuko naiz. Ez aiz bizi izango biotz zurbilleko beldurrari gezur diola esateko ta ostotsa gora-bera lo egiteko.

Ostotsak. Koroedun mutiko bat agertzen da, eskuan adar bat daukana

Nor dugu,
errege-ondoreko bat iduri,
sutitu ta bere aur-bekoki gaiñean
nagusitzaren koroia daroan ori?

GUZIAK. Adi zak ta ez egiok itzik.

Irugarren Agerpena. Izan adi leoi bat; arroki adi ta ez axolatu ire aurka aserretzen, sumintzen eta elkartzen diranai buruz. Ez dute iñoiz ere Macbeth garaituko Birnam'eko baso aundia Dusinane'ko muru goratura aren aurka etorri arte.

Descends

MACBETH. That will never be
Who can impress the forest, bid the tree
Unfix his earth-bound root? Sweet bodements! good!
Rebellion's head, rise never till the wood
Of Birnam rise, and our high-placed Macbeth
Shall live the lease of nature, pay his breath
To time and mortal custom. Yet my heart
Throbs to know one thing: tell me, if your art
Can tell so much: shall Banquo's issue ever
Reign in this kingdom?

ALL. Seek to know no more.

MACBETH. I will be satisfied: deny me this,
And an eternal curse fall on you! Let me know.
Why sinks that cauldron? and what noise is this?

Hautboys

First Witch. Show!

Second Witch. Show!

Third Witch. Show!

ALL. Show his eyes, and grieve his heart;
Come like shadows, so depart!

A show of Eight Kings, the last with a glass in his hand; GHOST OF BANQUO following

MACBETH. Thou art too like the spirit of Banquo: down!
Thy crown does sear mine eye-balls. And thy hair,
Thou other gold-bound brow, is like the first.
A third is like the former. Filthy hags!
Why do you show me this? A fourth! Start, eyes!
What, will the line stretch out to the crack of doom?
Another yet! A seventh! I'll see no more:
And yet the eighth appears, who bears a glass

Beratsen da

MACBETH. Egun eta eguzki es diteke ori. Nork eragin lezaioke basoari, aien zustraiak lurpetik idoki ditzatela zugatzei agindu ta? Aztiantza gozoa! Matxinada, ez goititu burua Birnam'eko oiana ibilli dedin arte ta gure Macbeth garaia bere gizon epea bizi izango da, bere zorra ilkorren aldian eta oituraz ordaintzen dularik. Ene biotza, ordea, bete gauza bat jakiteko irrikitzen dago. Ezaidazute baldin zuen antzea orrenbesteraiñokoa ba'da, Banquo'ren jatorria errege izango da erri ontan?

GUZIAK. Ez galdetu geiago.

MACBETH. Asebeterik gelditu nai dut. Baldin au ukatzen ba'didazute, betiko madarikatuak izan zaitetela! Jakin dezadan! Zergatik ondoratzen da pertz ori? Nolako soiñua dugu ori?

Zaamiolak

Lenengo Sorgiña. Agertu!

Bigarren Sorgiña. Agertu!

Irugarren Sorgiña. Agertu!

GUZIAK. Agertu bere aurrean, bere gogoa illundu; zatozte itzalak antzo, ta orrela aienatu!

Zortzi errege agertzen dira, bana-banaka dioazenak antzeztokian zear; azkenekoa, ispillu bat eskuan daukala BANQUO da, aiei jarraitzen

MACBETH. Banquo'ren mamuaren antzekoegia aiz. Ken! Ire koroiak nire betseiña kiskaltzen dik. Ta ire adatsa, beste urreko buruntsa batekin, lenengoarena bezelakoa duk. Irugarren bat lengoaren antzekoa duk. Sorgin satsuok! Zertako erakusten didazute au? Laugarren bat? Zapart egizute, ene begiok! Zer, lerroa luzatzen al duk Azken Auziaren turuta otserarte? Beste bat oraindik? Zazpigarren bat? Ez dut geiagorik ikusi nai! Ta zortzigarrena ere agertzen

Which shows me many more; and some I see
That two-fold balls and treble scepters carry:
Horrible sight! Now, I see, 'tis true;
For the blood-bolter'd Banquo smiles upon me,
And points at them for his.

Apparitions vanish

What, is this so?

First Witch. Ay, sir, all this is so: but why
Stands Macbeth thus amazedly?
Come, sisters, cheer we up his sprites,
And show the best of our delights:
I'll charm the air to give a sound,
While you perform your antic round:
That this great king may kindly say,
Our duties did his welcome pay.

Music. The witches dance and then vanish, with HECATE

MACBETH. Where are they? Gone? Let this pernicious hour
Stand aye accursed in the calendar!
Come in, without there!

Enter LENNOX

LENNOX. What's your grace's will?

MACBETH. Saw you the weird sisters?

LENNOX. No, my lord.

MACBETH. Came they not by you?

LENNOX. No, indeed, my lord.

MACBETH. Infected be the air whereon they ride;
And damn'd all those that trust them! I did hear
The galloping of horse: who was't came by?

da beste asko geiago erakusten dizkidan ispillua eramaten duna. Ta koroi bikoitz eta urre-zigor irukoitzak daramazkiten batzu ere ikusten ditut. Ikuskari izugarria! Orain ba-dakust egia dala Banquo odolduak parrezirri egiten baitit, beatzaz erakusten dizkidala beregandikoak bezela.

Agerpenak desagertzen dira

Zer, orrela al da ori?

Lenengo Sorgiña. Bai, jauna, guzi au onela da. Baiña zer dala ta Macbeth orren arriturik gelditzen da? Zatozte, aizpak; aren gogoa alaitu ta gure xorraldi obeak erakutsi ditzaiogun. Aizea sorestatuko dut soiñu bat sortu dedin zuen antziñeko inguru-dantza egiten duzuteiño. Errege aundi onek esan dezakela ongi-etorria begirunez esan diogula.

Soiñua. Sorgiñak dantzan eta itzali egiten dira

MACBETH. Nun dira? Joanak? Ordu gaizkor au madarikatua geldi dadilla egutegian!
Sar zaitez, kanpoan zauden ori!

LENNOX sartzen da

LENNOX. Zer nai duzu, errege jauna?

MACBETH. Aizpa aztiak ikusi al dituzu?

LENNOX. Ez, jauna.

MACBETH. Ez al ziran igaro zure ondotik?

LENNOX. Ez, jauna, egiaz.

MACBETH. Kutsutu dedila zaldikatzen ari diran aizea ta madarikatua aiek ziñesten dituna. Zaldi lauroinka otsa entzun irudi zait. Iñor eldu al da?

LENNOX. 'Tis two or three, my lord, that bring you word
Macduff is fled to England.

MACBETH. Fled to England!

LENNOX. Ay, my good lord.

MACBETH. Time, thou anticipatest my dread exploits:
The flighty purpose never is o'ertook
Unless the deed go with it; from this moment
The very firstlings of my heart shall be
The firstlings of my hand. And even now,
To crown my thoughts with acts, be it thought and done:
The castle of Macduff I will surprise;
Seize upon Fife; give to the edge o' the sword
His wife, his babes, and all unfortunate souls
That trace him in his line. No boasting like a fool;
This deed I'll do before this purpose cool.
But no more sights!—Where are these gentlemen?
Come, bring me where they are.

Exeunt

Scene 2

Fife. MACDUFF's castle.

Enter LADY MACDUFF, her Son, and ROSS

LADY MACDUFF. What had he done, to make him fly the land?

ROSS. You must have patience, madam.

LADY MACDUFF. He had none:
His flight was madness: when our actions do not,
Our fears do make us traitors.

ROSS. You know not
Whether it was his wisdom or his fear.

LENNOX. Bizpairu, jauna, Macduff'ek Ingelanda'ra iges egin dulako berriaz.

MACBETH. Ingelanda'ra iges egin dula?

LENNOX. Bai, jaun ona.

MACBETH. Aldi orrek, zuk uts eragiten diezu nire egikizun beldurgarriai! Asmo itzurtiak bein ere ez dira atzitzen, egitea aiekin ez ba'doa. Aurrerantzean, biotzaren asikiñak eskuaren asikiñak ere izango zazkit. Etu oraintxetik nire gogoetak egintzaz burutu dezaten, zer esan ta ura egin. Macduff'en gaztelua itsumustuan artu, Fife atzitu ta aren emaztea, aurrak ta aren askaziko jarraile errukarri guziak ezpata sorbatzari emango diet. Parrasteririk ez. Egintza asmoa otzitu baiño len bururatuko da. Ez, ordea, ikuskari geiagorik! [Goraki]. Nun dira zaldun oriek? Zatoste, eraman nazazute aiengana.

Irtetzen dira

2'garren agerraldia

Fife. MACDUFF'en gaztelua.

MACDUFF'en ANDREA. Bere semea ta ROSS sartzen dira

MACDUFF ANDREA. Zer egin ote du errialdetik iges egiteko?

ROSS. Egonarri izan bear duzu, andrea.

MACDUFF ANDREA. Berak ez du izan.
Bere igesa zorakeria izan da. Gure egipenek ez eta gure beldurrek egiten gaitut etoiak.

ROSS. Ez dakizu zer izan dan,
zugurtza ala beldurra.

LADY MACDUFF. Wisdom! to leave his wife, to leave his babes,
His mansion and his titles in a place
From whence himself does fly? He loves us not;
He wants the natural touch: for the poor wren,
The most diminutive of birds, will fight,
Her young ones in her nest, against the owl.
All is the fear and nothing is the love;
As little is the wisdom, where the flight
So runs against all reason.

ROSS. My dearest coz,
I pray you, school yourself: but for your husband,
He is noble, wise, judicious, and best knows
The fits o' the season. I dare not speak
much further;
But cruel are the times, when we are traitors
And do not know ourselves, when we hold rumour
From what we fear, yet know not what we fear,
But float upon a wild and violent sea
Each way and move. I take my leave of you:
Shall not be long but I'll be here again:
Things at the worst will cease, or else climb upward
To what they were before. My pretty cousin,
Blessing upon you!

LADY MACDUFF. Father'd he is, and yet he's fatherless.

ROSS. I am so much a fool, should I stay longer,
It would be my disgrace and your discomfort:
I take my leave at once.

Exit

LADY MACDUFF. Sirrah, your father's dead;
And what will you do now? How will you live?

Son. As birds do, mother.

LADY MACDUFF. What, with worms and flies?

Son. With what I get, I mean; and so do they.

MACDUFF ANDREA. Zugurtza! Berak iges egiten dion lekuan, emaztea, semeak, etxea, deiturak bertan bera utzi? Ez, ez gaitu maite; ez du biotzondorik. Epetxa, txorietan txikiena, burrukatuko da untzaren aurka bere kabiko kumeen alde. Beldur geiegi, maitasunik eza ta zugurtza gutxi da igesak gogamen guzia orrenbesteraiño jotzen dunean.

ROSS. Ene lengusiña maite orrek, zure burua zentzatu arren. Senarra, zintzo, zugur eta zentzuduna duzu ta ongi ezagunak ditu aldi auen zalapartak. Ez dut bekoki geiago esateko, baiña aldiak ankerrak dira gerok jakiteke etoiak geranean; zeren beldur geran ez jakin eta beldur izateko gure zera ba-dugula dakigunean, itsaso aserre ta gogor baten gaiñean ara ta ona iñarika ari geranean. Agur egiten dizut; luzaro gabe itzuliko naiz. Gauzak, txarrenera eldu ezkero, beratu ala lengoratu egiten dira. Ene lengusu ederra, Jainkoak bedeinka zaitzala!

MACDUFF ANDREA. Ba-du aita ta aita gabea da alaber.

ROSS. Zentzugabea naiz luzaroago ekuratu ezkero nire burua galdu ta auek galbidean sartu egingo nuke ta. Berberean uzten zaituztet.

ROSS irtetzen da

MACDUFF ANDREA. Txikitxo, ire aita il duk. Zer egingo orain? Nola biziko?

Semea. Txoriak bezela, ama.

MACDUFF ANDREA. Zer, arrez eta euliz?

Semea. Arki dezadanaz esan nai dut, aiek egiten dutenez.

LADY MACDUFF. Poor bird! Thou'ldst never fear the net nor lime,
The pitfall nor the gin.

Son. Why should I, mother? Poor birds they are not set for.
My father is not dead, for all your saying.

LADY MACDUFF. Yes, he is dead; how wilt thou do for a father?

Son. Nay, how will you do for a husband?

LADY MACDUFF. Why, I can buy me twenty at any market.

Son. Then you'll buy 'em to sell again.

LADY MACDUFF. Thou speak'st with all thy wit: and yet, i' faith,
With wit enough for thee.

Son. Was my father a traitor, mother?

LADY MACDUFF. Ay, that he was.

Son. What is a traitor?

LADY MACDUFF. Why, one that swears and lies.

Son. And be all traitors that do so?

LADY MACDUFF. Every one that does so is a traitor, and must be hanged.

Son. And must they all be hanged that swear and lie?

LADY MACDUFF. Every one.

Son. Who must hang them?

LADY MACDUFF. Why, the honest men.

MACDUFF ANDREA. Txoritxo gaisoa! Ez al aiz arte, lakio, lika naiz sareen beldur izango?

Semea. Zergatik ama? Aiek ez dira txori apalentzat jartzen. Aita ez da il, diozuna diozula.

MACDUFF ANDREA. Bai, illik zegok. Zer egingo duk aita bat arkitzeko?

Semea. Eta zuk zeuk zelan egingo dozu senartzakoa?

MACDUFF ANDREA. Nik edozein merkatutan ogei erosi nayeikezak.

Semea. Olan izatekotan barriro saltzeko erosiko dozuz.

MACDUFF ANDREA. Sentzun andiz itz egiten dok eta, egitan, iretzako sentzun geyegiz.

Semea. Nire aita etoya (saltzallea) ete zan, amatxo?

MACDUFF ANDREA. Bai, etoya zoan.

Semea. Zer da etoya?

MACDUFF ANDREA. Zin-egin eta guzurra esaten dauena.

Semea. Eta ori egiten daben guztiak etoyak ete dira?

MACDUFF ANDREA. Ori egiten dauen oro etoya dok, eta eskegi egin bear litzatekek.

Semea. Eta zin-egin eta guzurra esaten daben oro eskegi egin bear ete dira?

MACDUFF ANDREA. Guzti-gutiak.

Semea. Nok eskegi bear dauz?

MACDUFF ANDREA. Nok, gizon zintzoak ez bestek?

Son. Then the liars and swearers are fools,
for there are liars and swearers enow to beat
the honest men and hang up them.

LADY MACDUFF. Now, God help thee, poor monkey!
But how wilt thou do for a father?

Son. If he were dead, you'ld weep for
him: if you would not, it were a good sign
that I should quickly have a new father.

LADY MACDUFF. Poor prattler, how thou talk'st!

Enter a Messenger

Messenger. Bless you, fair dame! I am not to you known,
Though in your state of honour I am perfect.
I doubt some danger does approach you nearly:
If you will take a homely man's advice,
Be not found here; hence, with your little ones.
To fright you thus, methinks, I am too savage;
To do worse to you were fell cruelty,
Which is too nigh your person. Heaven preserve you!
I dare abide no longer.

Exit

LADY MACDUFF. Whither should I fly?
I have done no harm. But I remember now
I am in this earthly world; where to do harm
Is often laudable, to do good sometime
Accounted dangerous folly: why then, alas,
Do I put up that womanly defence,
To say I have done no harm?

Enter Murderers

What are these faces?

First Murderer. Where is your husband?

Semea. Ori olan ba'da, guzurtiak eta zin-egilleak zoroak dira, eta izan be, guzurti ta zin-egillerik asko dago zintzoak benderatu ta eskegiteko.

MACDUFF ANDREA. Orain Yaungoikoa lagun akik, tximinotxo orreri! Baña nolan yokatuko dok aitarik ezean.

Semea. Il ba'litz, negar egingo genuke ura zala bide. Baldin negar ez ba'dagizu, aita berri bat laster laster eukiko dudalako ezupide ona da.

MACDUFF ANDREA. Berritsu gaiso ori, bai mintzatzen aizela!

Geznari bat sartzen da

Geznari. Jainkoak onetsi zaitzala, andre uren ori! Ez nauzu ezagutzen, nik zure mail garaia ezagutzen dudan arren. Galbide bat urbiltzen ote zaizun beldur naiz. Gizon apal baten esana onartu nai ba-duzu, ez ekuratu emen; iges egizu zure aurrakin. Zu onela izutuaz basatiegi naiz, nik uste; gaizkiago litzake, ordea, orren urbil duzun ankerkeri aundiaren berririk zuri ez ematea. Jainkoak lagun dagizula. Ez naiz ausartzen luzaroago egoten.

Geznaria irtetzen da.

MACDUFF ANDREA. Nora iges negike? Ez dut kalterik egin. Orain oroitzen naiz, ordea, lurraren gaiñean naizela, ta emen gaizki egitea goresgarria da sarri. ta ongi egitea zorakeri galbidetsua batzutan. Zertako, beraz, emakume zuribide au aurkeztu. "Ez dut gaizkirik egin?"

Eriotzegileak sartzen dira

Nolako itxurak dira oriek?

Eriotzegille. Nun duzu senarra?

LADY MACDUFF. I hope, in no place so unsanctified
Where such as thou mayst find him.

First Murderer. He's a traitor.

Son. Thou liest, thou shag-hair'd villain!

First Murderer. What, you egg!

Stabbing him

Young fry of treachery!

Son. He has kill'd me, mother:
Run away, I pray you!

Dies

Exit LADY MACDUFF, crying "Murder!"

Exeunt Murderers, following her

Scene 3

England. Before the King's palace

Enter MALCOLM and MACDUFF

MALCOLM. Let us seek out some desolate shade, and there
Weep our sad bosoms empty.

MACDUFF. Let us rather
Hold fast the mortal sword, and like good men
Bestride our down-fall'n birthdom: each new morn
New widows howl, new orphans cry, new sorrows
Strike heaven on the face, that it resounds
As if it felt with Scotland and yell'd out
Like syllable of dolour.

MACDUFF ANDREA. Zu bezelakoakin buruz-buru egin dezaken leku ain dongean ez, nik uste.

Eriotzegille. Etoi bat da!

Semea. Gezur diok, zital, belarri illetsu orrek!

Eriotzegille. Arrautz ori!

Sastakatzen du

Etoikume ori!

Semea. Il nau, ama;
igesi, igesi, arren!

Iltzen da

MACDUFF ANDREA irtetzen da "Eriotzegille!" deadarka

Eriotzegilleak jarraitzen zaie

3'garren agerraldia

Ingelanda'n. Errege-jauregiaren aurrean.

MALCOLM eta MACDUFF sartzen dira.

MALCOLM. Billa dezagun itzalpe illun bat eta an negar dagigun gure biotz goibelok lasaitu arte.

MACDUFF. Ar dezagun, aitzitik, ezpata sarraskitzaillea ta babes dezagun gizonki gure jaioterri eroria. Goiz berri bakoitzean alargun berriak zinkurinka ari dira, umezurtz berriak deadarka ta min berriek jotzen dute Eskotelanda'rekin mindu ta arekin oiñazezko oiu bera egiten bai'lun, burrunbaka ari dan zeruko aurpegia.

MALCOLM. What I believe I'll wail,
What know believe, and what I can redress,
As I shall find the time to friend, I will.
What you have spoke, it may be so perchance.
This tyrant, whose sole name blisters our tongues,
Was once thought honest: you have loved him well.
He hath not touch'd you yet. I am young;
but something
You may deserve of him through me, and wisdom
To offer up a weak poor innocent lamb
To appease an angry god.

MACDUFF. I am not treacherous.

MALCOLM. But Macbeth is.
A good and virtuous nature may recoil
In an imperial charge. But I shall crave your pardon;
That which you are my thoughts cannot transpose:
Angels are bright still, though the brightest fell;
Though all things foul would wear the brows of grace,
Yet grace must still look so.

MACDUFF. I have lost my hopes.

MALCOLM. Perchance even there where I did find my doubts.
Why in that rawness left you wife and child,
Those precious motives, those strong knots of love,
Without leave-taking? I pray you,
Let not my jealousies be your dishonours,
But mine own safeties. You may be rightly just,
Whatever I shall think.

MACDUFF. Bleed, bleed, poor country!
Great tyranny! lay thou thy basis sure,
For goodness dare not cheque thee: wear thou thy wrongs;
The title is affeer'd! Fare thee well, lord:
I would not be the villain that thou think'st
For the whole space that's in the tyrant's grasp,
And the rich East to boot.

MALCOLM. Ziñetsi dezadana deitoratuko dut, jatin dezadana ziñetsiko ta mugona datorrenean zuzendu litekena zuzenduko. Esan duzuna egia da, bearbada, baiña izen utsaz mingaiña maskuilluz betetzen saigun tiranu ori zintzotzat artua zan eta zerorrek maite izan zenun. Ez dizu oraiño ezer ere egin. Gaztea naiz, baiña aren ederra irabazi zenezake nire onez. Zugurtza da bildots gaiso, aul, errugabe bat eskeintzea Jainko baten aserrea gozatzeko.

MACDUFF. Ez nauzu etoi.

MALCOLM. Macbeth ba-da, ordea. Gogo on eta ontzale bat añor egin lezaioke erregeren agindu bateri; baiña barka eske nagokizu. Nire gogoetak zerana ezin alda dezake. Aingeruek beti dirdiratzen dute, dirdiratsuena erori ba'zan ere. Pekatuak santutasunaren aurpegia bera artuko ba'lu, ori ta guzti ere, santutasunak beti irudiko litzake dan bezela.

MACDUFF. Nire itxaropenak gald nitun.

MALCOLM. Nire zalantzak arkitu nitun lekuan, nunbait. Zergatik utzi dituzu orren itoka emazte ta aurrak, gure maitasunaren bultzagai bikain eta korapillo indartsu oriek, aiei agurrik esan gabe? Ikus itzazu, arren, nire zalantzetan, ez zuretzako iraiñak, nire segurantza baiño. Gizon egitia izan zaitekez, nire ustea dana dala.

MACDUFF. Odolustu adi, odolustu, erri gaiso ori! Nausikeri altsu ori, sendotu adi ire oiñarrian onbideak ez baitu bekokirik ire aurka egiteko. Eramazkik ire gaitzak errege-aulkiaren jabegaia beldur dalako. Ongi izan, jauna. Ez nuke uste duzun doillorra izan nai, tiranuaren erpetan dagon lurralde osoa ta Sortzalde aberatsaren orde ere.

MALCOLM. Be not offended:
I speak not as in absolute fear of you.
I think our country sinks beneath the yoke;
It weeps, it bleeds; and each new day a gash
Is added to her wounds: I think withal
There would be hands uplifted in my right;
And here from gracious England have I offer
Of goodly thousands: but, for all this,
When I shall tread upon the tyrant's head,
Or wear it on my sword, yet my poor country
Shall have more vices than it had before,
More suffer and more sundry ways than ever,
By him that shall succeed.

MACDUFF. What should he be?

MALCOLM. It is myself I mean: in whom I know
All the particulars of vice so grafted
That, when they shall be open'd, black Macbeth
Will seem as pure as snow, and the poor state
Esteem him as a lamb, being compared
With my confineless harms.

MACDUFF. Not in the legions
Of horrid hell can come a devil more damn'd
In evils to top Macbeth.

MALCOLM. I grant him bloody,
Luxurious, avaricious, false, deceitful,
Sudden, malicious, smacking of every sin
That has a name: but there's no bottom, none,
In my voluptuousness: your wives, your daughters,
Your matrons and your maids, could not fill up
The cistern of my lust, and my desire
All continent impediments would o'erbear
That did oppose my will: better Macbeth
Than such an one to reign.

MACDUFF. Boundless intemperance
In nature is a tyranny; it hath been
The untimely emptying of the happy throne

MALCOLM. Ez zaitez gaitzitu. Ez dut onela itz egiten zurekiko gibel-beldurrarren. Uste dut gure aberria uztarri pean ondatzen dala; negar egiten du, odolustutzen da, ta egun bakoitzean zauri gaiñeratzen die aren sakaillai. Uste dut ere eskuak goratuko lirakela nire eskubideen alde ta emen Ingelanda'ko errege garaiak ainbat milla gudari eskeiñi dizkit. Baiña ala ta guzti ere, tiranuaren burua oin pean naiz ezpata muturrean ba'neuka ere, ene aberri gaisoak len baiño keri geiago izango lituke; geiago ta iñoiz baiño bide geiagotan miñartuko luke aren jarraillearen pean.

MACDUFF. Zer izango litzate ura?

MALCOLM. Neronetzat naiz mintzatzen. Keri-mota guziak onen errostatuak baditut eta zabalki agertuko lirakenean, Macbeth beltzak elurra bezain garbia lirudike, ta erri gaisoak bildots batetzat joko luke nire gaiztakeri mugagabearekin erkatzean.

MACDUFF. Inpernu ikaracarriaren taldeetan ez dago Macbeth bezainbateko deabru gaizkiñik.

MALCOLM. Izan ere, ba-da odolkoi, aragikor, gezurxuri, zeken, etoi, gaizto, sakerre ta izen bat dun edozein keriz kutsatua. Burla nire lizunkeria ondo-gabea da, bai, ondogabea. Zuen emazteak, auen alabak, zuen etxekoandreak eta zuen neskatxek ezin lezakete bete nire aragikeriaren osiña ta nire irritsak nire naiaren aurkako eragozpen guziak lurreratuko lituke. Obe Macbeth orrelako erregea baiño!

MACDUFF. Muga gabeko irritsa tiranu bat da guretzat. Ura izan dala ta jauralki zoriontsuak ustu ta errege

And fall of many kings. But fear not yet
To take upon you what is yours: you may
Convey your pleasures in a spacious plenty,
And yet seem cold, the time you may so hoodwink.
We have willing dames enough: there cannot be
That vulture in you, to devour so many
As will to greatness dedicate themselves,
Finding it so inclined.

MALCOLM. With this there grows
In my most ill-composed affection such
A stanchless avarice that, were I king,
I should cut off the nobles for their lands,
Desire his jewels and this other's house:
And my more-having would be as a sauce
To make me hunger more; that I should forge
Quarrels unjust against the good and loyal,
Destroying them for wealth.

MACDUFF. This avarice
Sticks deeper, grows with more pernicious root
Than summer-seeming lust, and it hath been
The sword of our slain kings: yet do not fear;
Scotland hath foisons to fill up your will.
Of your mere own: all these are portable,
With other graces weigh'd.

MALCOLM. But I have none: the king-becoming graces,
As justice, verity, temperance, stableness,
Bounty, perseverance, mercy, lowliness,
Devotion, patience, courage, fortitude,
I have no relish of them, but abound
In the division of each several crime,
Acting it many ways. Nay, had I power, I should
Pour the sweet milk of concord into hell,
Uproar the universal peace, confound
All unity on earth.

MACDUFF. O Scotland, Scotland!

MALCOLM. If such a one be fit to govern, speak:
I am as I have spoken.

asko erori egin dira bear baiño len. Baiña, ez izan beldurrik zure dana zureganatzeko. Irritsa ase dezakezu ta otz iduri, gizarteari iruzur egiñaz. Badugu andere oldetsurik aski. Ezin diteke bizi dan saiak zure leia ori dala ikusi dezatenean eskeiñiko zaizun aiña irenstea.

MALCOLM. Orren gain, nire izakera guziz gaiztoan dirugose ain ase-eziña geitzen da ta errege ba'nintz, aundikiei bizia kenduko nieke aien lurrak niretzeko. Onen pitxiak ata aren etxeak irrikatuko nituke; ta areago eukitzea goseago izateko bazi bat nuke; ordun eztabaida bidegabeak asmatuko nituke on eta kirmenen aurka aiek ondatuz ni aberastutzeko.

MACDUFF. Diru gose orrek barrurago sartu ta erro kaltetsuagoak egiten ditu uda lore dan aragikeriak baiño; gure erregeak sarraskitu ditun ezpata izan da. Baiña ez izan beldurrik. Eskotelanda'k ba-dauka eskuartea zure naia betetzeko zure ogasunaz soillik. Guzi ori jasankorra da beste onbide batzukin ordetuta.

MALCOLM. Baiñan ez dut bat ere. Erregeai dagozkien onbideak, zuzentasuna, egia, neurtona, sendotasuna, ontasuna, irautasuna, errukia, errukiortasuna, jainkozaletasuna, egonarria, kemena, indarra ez dira nire gogarako baiña ba-dut eskuartea txarbide batean ari izan nai dudanean eta amaika bidez egiten dut. Bai, eskubidea ba'un, irizkidetasunaren gozoa inpernuan isuriko nuke gizarteko bakea lardaskatuko, lur gaiñeko batasun guzia nastuko.

MACDUFF. Oi, Eskotelanda, Eskotelanda!

MALCOLM. Orrelako gizona nagusi izateko egokia ba'da, mintza. Esan dudana nauzu.

MACDUFF. Fit to govern!
No, not to live. O nation miserable,
With an untitled tyrant bloody-scepter'd,
When shalt thou see thy wholesome days again,
Since that the truest issue of thy throne
By his own interdiction stands accursed,
And does blaspheme his breed? Thy royal father
Was a most sainted king: the queen that bore thee,
Oftener upon her knees than on her feet,
Died every day she lived. Fare thee well!
These evils thou repeat'st upon thyself
Have banish'd me from Scotland. O my breast,
Thy hope ends here!

MALCOLM. Macduff, this noble passion,
Child of integrity, hath from my soul
Wiped the black scruples, reconciled my thoughts
To thy good truth and honour. Devilish Macbeth
By many of these trains hath sought to win me
Into his power, and modest wisdom plucks me
From over-credulous haste: but God above
Deal between thee and me! for even now
I put myself to thy direction, and
Unspeak mine own detraction, here abjure
The taints and blames I laid upon myself,
For strangers to my nature. I am yet
Unknown to woman, never was forsworn,
Scarcely have coveted what was mine own,
At no time broke my faith, would not betray
The devil to his fellow and delight
No less in truth than life: my first false speaking
Was this upon myself: what I am truly,
Is thine and my poor country's to command:
Whither indeed, before thy here-approach,
Old Siward, with ten thousand warlike men,
Already at a point, was setting forth.
Now we'll together; and the chance of goodness
Be like our warranted quarrel! Why are you silent?

MACDUFF. Nagusi izateko egokia! Ez, bizi izateko ere ez. Erri kupigarri ori, tiranu batek osturiko urre-zigor odelduaren azpian jarria! Noiz birrikusiko duzu osasun-eguna, ire jauralkiaren jabegai jatorrenak berak beraren buruari eskubidea kendu ta bere odolari birao egiten ba'dio? Zure aita erregea, gure erregeen gurenetako bat zan; eta sabelean eraman ziñun erregiña, geiagotan belauniko zutik baiño, abere biziaren egun bakoitzean il zan. Agur, ba! Zure buruari ezartzen dizkiozun gaitzak Eskotelanda'tik arroztu naute. Ene biotz au, emen galdu duk ire itxarobidea!

MALCOLM. Macduff, osotasunaren kumea dan zirrara zintzo orrek ene gogoaren susmo beltzak ezabatu ta nire bulkoak zure kirmetasun eta zintasunarekin elkartzen ditu berriz. Macbeth deabru orrek, orrelako amarrukerien bidez ni bere eskuperatzeko alegiñak egiten ditu ta zugurtza naurridun batek lasterregi ziñestea eragozten dit. Baiña Jainkoa buru izan dezagula gure artu-emanetan! Oraintxetik artzen baitzaitut ots-emaile, nire buruari ezarri diodan gaitza gezurtatzen dut eta nire buruari egotzi dizkiodan salakuntza ta laidoak ukatzen ditut, nire izakeraganako arrotzak bezela. Ez dut oraiño emakumerik ezautu, ez naiz bein ere ziñausle izan eta neronena dana doi-doi irrikatu dut. Ez dut egundaiño nire itza jan, ez ta ez nioke deabrua beste deabru pera emango; ta egia bizia aiña maite dut. Nire lengo gezurra nire aurka oraintsu esan dudana da. Egiz naizena zure ta nire aberri gaisoaren agindu pean duzute. Izan ere, zure onaratzea baiño len, Siward zarra, amar milla gudari gertu ta ornitukin, bideari ekitear zegon. Orain elkarrekin joango gera ta gure ondore onaren zoria gure auziaren zuzentasuna bezain aundia izango al da! Zer dala ta isilik zaude?

MACDUFF. Such welcome and unwelcome things at once
'Tis hard to reconcile.

Enter a doctor

MALCOLM. Well; more anon.—Comes the king forth, I pray you?

Doctor. Ay, sir; there are a crew of wretched souls
That stay his cure: their malady convinces
The great assay of art; but at his touch—
Such sanctity hath heaven given his hand—
They presently amend.

MALCOLM. I thank you, doctor.

Exit Doctor

MACDUFF. What's the disease he means?

MALCOLM. 'Tis call'd the evil:
A most miraculous work in this good king;
Which often, since my here-remain in England,
I have seen him do. How he solicits heaven,
Himself best knows: but strangely-visited people,
All swoln and ulcerous, pitiful to the eye,
The mere despair of surgery, he cures,
Hanging a golden stamp about their necks,
Put on with holy prayers: and 'tis spoken,
To the succeeding royalty he leaves
The healing benediction. With this strange virtue,
He hath a heavenly gift of prophecy,
And sundry blessings hang about his throne,
That speak him full of grace.

Enter ROSS

MACDUFF. See, who comes here?

MALCOLM. My countryman; but yet I know him not.

MACDUFF. Onenbeste atsegin eta atsegabe erabatean elkartzea nekeza da.

Osagille bat sartzen da

MALCOLM. Itz egingo dugu bereala. Errege agertuko al da?

Osagille. Bai, jauna; ba-dauka gisagaiso talde bat osasun zai. Aien eritasunak antzearen alegin guziak garaitzen ditute; baiña ikutzen ditunekoxe—Jainkoak aren eskuai orrelako gurentasuna eman die ta—berealaxe osatzen dira.

MALCOLM. Anitz esker, osagille jauna.

Osagille irtetzen da

MACDUFF. Zein eritasun da ori?

MALCOLM. Errege-miña diotsate. Errege zintzo onen lan miragarria da, ta Ingelanda'ra etorri nintzanetik batzutan ikusi diot egiten. Nola beartzen dun zerua iñork ez daki berak baizik, baiña miñantz bakanek larritutako lagunak, puztuak eta zaurituak, begiratzeko errukigarriak, eri etsiak osatzen ditu urrezko medailla bat lepotik aiei eskegiz otoitz gurenak esaten ditularik. Utziko omen die jarraituko zaizkion erregeai osatzeko eskerra ori. Onindar onekin ba-du ereigarle antze jainkozkoa, ta aren jauralkia inguratzen duten onespen ugariek eskerrez beterik dagola darakuste.

ROSS sartzen da.

MACDUFF. Ikusazu nor datorkigun.

MALCOLM. Nire aberkide bat; baiña ez dut ezautzen.

MACDUFF. My ever-gentle cousin, welcome hither.

MALCOLM. I know him now. Good God, betimes remove
The means that makes us strangers!

ROSS. Sir, amen.

MACDUFF. Stands Scotland where it did?

ROSS. Alas, poor country!
Almost afraid to know itself. It cannot
Be call'd our mother, but our grave; where nothing,
But who knows nothing, is once seen to smile;
Where sighs and groans and shrieks that rend the air
Are made, not mark'd; where violent sorrow seems
A modern ecstasy; the dead man's knell
Is there scarce ask'd for who; and good men's lives
Expire before the flowers in their caps,
Dying or ere they sicken.

MACDUFF. O, relation
Too nice, and yet too true!

MALCOLM. What's the newest grief?

ROSS. That of an hour's age doth hiss the speaker:
Each minute teems a new one.

MACDUFF. How does my wife?

ROSS. Why, well.

MACDUFF. And all my children?

ROSS. Well too.

MACDUFF. The tyrant has not batter'd at their peace?

MACDUFF. Nire lengusu maite, ongi etorria.

MALCOLM. Orain ezautzen dut. Jainko on orrek, urrutira ezazu laster elkarganako arrotz egiten gaituna!

ROSS. Ala biz.

MACDUFF. Bereartan dugu Eskotelanda?

ROSS. Ene, aberri gaisoa! Ozta-ozta ezautzen du bere burua. Ezin izendatu dezaiokegu ama, illobi baizik. Ezer ez dakianak baiño parrezirri egiten ez dun lurra; aieneak, zinkuriñak eta eguratsa urratzen duten karraisiak oartuak ez dirarn lekua; oiñaze gogorrenak noiznaiko biotz-ikaratzat artuak diran lekua. Il ezkillak jotzen du ta ez da galdetzen norengatik, eta gizon zintzoek beren kapelaetako loreak baiño gutxiago diraute oeratu gabe iltzen diralarik.

MACDUFF. Ori txosten zeatzegia ta egitiegia, ala ere!

MALCOLM. Zein da zorigabe berriena?

ROSS. Ordu batekoa zarra da iragartzen daneko, miñutu bakoitzak berri bat erditzen du ta.

MACDUFF. Nola dago nire emaztea?

ROSS. Ongi, ba.

MACDUFF. Ta bire aur guziak?

ROSS. Ongi ere.

MACDUFF. Tiranuak ez al du aien bakea nastu?

ROSS. No; they were well at peace when I did leave 'em.

MACDUFF. But not a niggard of your speech: how goes't?

ROSS. When I came hither to transport the tidings,
Which I have heavily borne, there ran a rumour
Of many worthy fellows that were out;
Which was to my belief witness'd the rather,
For that I saw the tyrant's power a-foot:
Now is the time of help; your eye in Scotland
Would create soldiers, make our women fight,
To doff their dire distresses.

MALCOLM. Be't their comfort
We are coming thither: gracious England hath
Lent us good Siward and ten thousand men;
An older and a better soldier none
That Christendom gives out.

ROSS. Would I could answer
This comfort with the like! But I have words
That would be howl'd out in the desert air,
Where hearing should not latch them.

MACDUFF. What concern they?
The general cause? or is it a fee-grief due to some single breast?

ROSS. No mind that's honest
But in it shares some woe; though the main part
Pertains to you alone.

MACDUFF. If it be mine,
Keep it not from me, quickly let me have it.

ROSS. Let not your ears despise my tongue for ever,
Which shall possess them with the heaviest sound
That ever yet they heard.

MACDUFF. Hum! I guess at it.

ROSS. Ez bake-baktetan zauden utzi nitunean.

MACDUFF. Ez zaitez orren itz-urri izan; zer berri?

ROSS. Ekartzen nitun berri larriak emateko
onara eldu nintzanean, lagun jator askok
izkilluak artu ditutelako zurrumurrua zebillan,
eta orixe ziñetsi dut tiranuaren gudari taldeak
gertutzen ari dirala ikusita. Au da lagun
etortzeko ordua. Zure begiak gudariak sortuko
lituke Eskotelanda'n, emakumeak ere eramango
lituke gudukara aien gaitz gogorrak kenerazteko.

MACOLM. Biotz izan dezatela. Ara
joko dugu. Ingelanda'ko errege onak
amar milla gizon eta Siward bioztuna
eman dizkit. Gudari zarrago ta oberik
ez dago kristotarren artean.

ROSS. Jainkoa'k ai letsa poz bideori
ainbatekoaz nik ordaintza! Belarri batek ere
artuko ez lituken eremuko aizetan ots egin
bearko lituketen itzak dira.

MACDUFF. Nori doazkio?
Guzien auziari? Ala biotz bakar baten min berezia da?

ROSS. Ez dago artan bere zatia ez
daukan gogo zindorik, aundiena,
ordea, zuri dagokizu.

MACDUFF. Nire ba'da,
ez gorde; euki dezadan bereala.

ROSS. Zure belarriek ez dezatela betiko
arbuiatu, egundaiño entzun dituten soiñu
larrienaz joko ditun nire mingaiña.

MACDUFF. Uf! Igartzen dut.

ROSS. Your castle is surprised; your wife and babes
Savagely slaughter'd: to relate the manner,
Were, on the quarry of these murder'd deer,
To add the death of you.

MALCOLM. Merciful heaven!
What, man! Ne'er pull your hat upon your brows;
Give sorrow words: the grief that does not speak
Whispers the o'er-fraught heart and bids it break.

MACDUFF. My children too?

ROSS. Wife, children, servants, all
That could be found.

MACDUFF. And I must be from thence!
My wife kill'd too?

ROSS. I have said.

MALCOLM. Be comforted:
Let's make us medicines of our great revenge,
To cure this deadly grief.

MACDUFF. He has no children. All my pretty ones?
Did you say all? O hell-kite! All?
What, all my pretty chickens and their dam
At one fell swoop?

MALCOLM. Dispute it like a man.

MACDUFF. I shall do so;
But I must also feel it as a man:
I cannot but remember such things were,
That were most precious to me. Did heaven look on,
And would not take their part? Sinful Macduff,
They were all struck for thee! naught that I am,
Not for their own demerits, but for mine,
Fell slaughter on their souls. Heaven rest them now!

ROSS. Zure gaztelua itsumustuan artu dute;
zure emazte ta aurrak sarraskitu ditute
aberekiro. Nola izan dan zuri esatea sakail
orri zure eriotza gaiñeratzea litzake.

MALCOLM. Jainko urrikaltsu ori!
Ots, gizona, ea sartu kapela begien gaiñean. Emazkiozu itzak miñari. Itzik egiten ez dun zorigaitza marmarka ari da biotz zamatuegian eta ausi dedilla agintzen dio.

MACDUFF. Ene aurrak ere?

ROSS. Emaztea, aurrak, otseiñak,
arkitu zitekean guzia.

MACDUFF. Ta ni aiengandik urrun!
Nire emaztea ere illa?

ROSS. Esan dut.

MALCOLM. Biotz on! Eta
asperkunde aundi bat izan dezagula
ongibide min eriogarri au osatzeko.

MACDUFF. Berak ez dauka aurrik! Ene aur polit guziak? Guziak esan duzu? Inpernuko miru ori! Guziak? Zer, ene txita polit guziak eta aien ama atzaparkada gogor batez arrapatuak?

MALCOLM. Ar ezazu gizon gisa.

MACDUFF. Egingo dut, bai; baiña gizon gisa min artu bear dut ere. Ezin aztu dezaket sorkari oriek bizi zirala, maite nitula, Zeruak ikusi al du ori ezaxolik? Macduff pekataria, zu zerala bide erori ziran guziak! Ene errukarri au!, ez aien erruengatik, nereengatik baizik, eriotzegiña erori zan aien gogoen gaiñen. Jainkoak eman dezaiela atsedena!

MALCOLM. Be this the whetstone of your sword: let grief
Convert to anger; blunt not the heart, enrage it.

MACDUFF. O, I could play the woman with mine eyes
And braggart with my tongue! But, gentle heavens,
Cut short all intermission; front to front
Bring thou this fiend of Scotland and myself;
Within my sword's length set him; if he 'scape,
Heaven forgive him too!

MALCOLM. This tune goes manly.
Come, go we to the king; our power is ready;
Our lack is nothing but our leave; Macbeth
Is ripe for shaking, and the powers above
Put on their instruments. Receive what cheer you may:
The night is long that never finds the day.

Exeunt

MALCOLM. Izan be di ori zure ezpata zorroztuko duzun deztera. Miña aserre biurtu bedi, ta biotza kamustu gabe, amurruz bete beza.

MACDUFF. O, emakumearena egin nezake negarraz eta kementsuarena mingaiña. Baiña, Jainko maitea, len-baiño-len izan dedilla! Jarri nazazu Eskotelanda'ko gaizkin orren aurrean, ekarri ezadazu ezpataren irispidean: baldin iges egiten ba'du, Jainkoa'k barka dezala ordun!

MALCOLM. Ori da gizonki mintzatzea. Zatoz, goazen errege ikustera. Gure gudaroztea gerturik dago ta ari agur egitea besterik ez dugu. Macbeth galzorian dago ta Goiko Aldunak ura iñarrosteko gertutzen dira. Ar ezazu poztu zaitzaken guzia. Ez dago gau ain luzerik eguna arki ez dezakenik.

Irtetzen dira

Act 5

Scene 1

Dunsinane. Ante-room in the castle.

Enter a Doctor of Physic and a Waiting-Gentlewoman

Doctor. I have two nights watched with you, but can perceive no truth in your report. When was it she last walked?

Gentlewoman. Since his majesty went into the field, I have seen her rise from her bed, throw her night-gown upon her, unlock her closet, take forth paper, fold it, write upon't, read it, afterwards seal it, and again return to bed; yet all this while in a most fast sleep.

Doctor. A great perturbation in nature, to receive at once the benefit of sleep, and do the effects of watching! In this slumbery agitation, besides her walking and other actual performances, what, at any time, have you heard her say?

Gentlewoman. That, sir, which I will not report after her.

Doctor. You may to me: and 'tis most meet you should.

Gentlewoman. Neither to you nor any one; having no witness to confirm my speech.

Enter LADY MACBETH, with a taper

Lo you, here she comes! This is her very guise; and, upon my life, fast asleep. Observe her; stand close.

Doctor. How came she by that light?

Gentlewoman. Why, it stood by her: she has light by her continually; 'tis her command.

5'garren atala

1'go agerraldia

Dunsinane. Gazteluko gela bat.

Osagille bat eta jauregiko andre bat

Osagille. Bi gautan beilatu naiz zurekin, baiña ezin izan dut sendetsi esan duzunaren egia. Noiz egurastu zan azken aldiz?

Andre. Errege jauna gudara joan zanetik ikusi dut oetik jeikitzen, bere gau-soiñekoa jantzi, bere idaz-maia iriki, papera atera, ura tolestu, artan idatzi, gero irakurri ta bereala oera itzultzen; guzi ori osoro lokarturik zegola.

Osagille. Izaeraren naspil aundia! Loaren on-egiña artu ta bat-batera ernai egoteari dagozkionak bururatu! Lo-ibilketa ortan, joan-etorriak eta beste egintzak bazterki utzita, zer entzun duzu esaten, bein-edo-bein?

Andre. Berriz esango ez dudana, jauna, aren ondoren.

Osagille. Ba-dezakezu niri ta oso egoki ere zaizu.

Andre. Ez zuri ez iñori ere, esaten dudana ziñeztatu dezaten lekukorik ez ba-dut.

MACBETH ANDREA sartzen da, arkai piztu batekin

Begira! or dator! Ori duzu bere oiturazko itxura ta, biziaren gain! osoro lokarturik dago. Gomazu; urbil zaitez.

Osagille. Nundik artu zun argi ori?

Andre. Bere ondean zeukan; beti dauka argia bere ondoan; bere agindua da.

Doctor. You see, her eyes are open.

Gentlewoman. Ay, but their sense is shut.

Doctor. What is it she does now? Look, how she rubs her hands.

Gentlewoman. It is an accustomed action with her, to seem thus washing her hands: I have known her continue in this a quarter of an hour.

LADY MACBETH. Yet here's a spot.

Doctor. Hark! she speaks: I will set down what comes from her, to satisfy my remembrance the more strongly.

LADY MACBETH. Out, damned spot! out, I say!—One: two: why, then, 'tis time to do't.—Hell is murky!—Fie, my lord, fie! a soldier, and afeard? What need we fear who knows it, when none can call our power to account?—Yet who would have thought the old man to have had so much blood in him.

Doctor. Do you mark that?

LADY MACBETH. The thane of Fife had a wife: where is she now?—
What, will these hands ne'er be clean?—No more o' that, my lord, no more o' that: you mar all with this starting.

Doctor. Go to, go to; you have known what you should not.

Gentlewoman. She has spoke what she should not, I am sure of that: heaven knows what she has known.

LADY MACBETH. Here's the smell of the blood still: all the perfumes of Arabia will not sweeten this little hand. Oh, oh, oh!

Doctor. What a sigh is there! The heart is sorely charged.

Osagille. Ikusazu bere begiak irikita dagoz.

Andre. Bai, baiña oarpenari itxiak.

Osagille. Zertan ari da orain? Ikus nola ikuzten ditun eskuak.

Andre. Oitura da ori egitea; eskuak
garbitzen ditulakoa. Ordu laurden batetan
ortan ari izatea ikusi dut.

MACBETH ANDREA. Oraindik ere ba-dago emen orban bat.

Osagille. Entzun, mintzatzen ari da. Idatziko dut esan dezan guzia nire gogoan obeki gordetzeko.

MACBETH ANDREA. Ut, orban madarikatu ori! Ut,
dasaizut! Bat, bi, ots, egiteke aldia eldu da. Inpernua
goibela da. Au lotsa, ene jauna, au lotsa! Gudari bat
izan eta beldur? Ezautu ba'dadi ere, guri zer iñork
gure almenari kontu artu ezin dezaiekelarik? Baiña,
ziñetsiko zun agure ark ainbeste odol zeukanik?

Osagille. Entzuten al duzu ori?

MACBETH ANDREA. Fife'ko thaneak ba-zeukan emazte bat;
nun da
orain? Baiña, zer! eskuok ez dira sekulan garbi egongo? Ez geiago orrelakorik, ene jauna, ez geiago orrelakorik; dana alperrik galtzen duzu izu-laborri oriekin.

Osagille. Zoaz, zoaz. Jakin bear ez zenukena dakizu.

Andre. Berak itz egin du bear ez lukena, etsita nago ortaz. Batek bada orrek esaten duna.

MACBETH ANDREA. Beti odol sunda. Arabi'ko
lurringai guziek ez liokete kutsua kenduko esku
txiki oni. Oi, oi,oi!

Osagille. Ori asperena! Biotza larriki zamatua dago.

Gentlewoman. I would not have such a heart in my bosom for the dignity of the whole body.

Doctor. Well, well, well,—

Gentlewoman. Pray God it be, sir.

Doctor. This disease is beyond my practise: yet I have known those which have walked in their sleep who have died holily in their beds.

LADY MACBETH. Wash your hands, put on your nightgown;
look not so
pale.—I tell you yet again, Banquo's buried; he
cannot come out on's grave.

Doctor. Even so?

LADY MACBETH. To bed, to bed! there's knocking at the gate:
come, come, come, come, give me your hand. What's
done cannot be undone.—To bed, to bed, to bed!

Exit

Doctor. Will she go now to bed?

Gentlewoman. Directly.

Doctor. Foul whisperings are abroad: unnatural deeds
Do breed unnatural troubles: infected minds
To their deaf pillows will discharge their secrets:
More needs she the divine than the physician.
God, God forgive us all! Look after her;
Remove from her the means of all annoyance,
And still keep eyes upon her. So, good night:
My mind she has mated, and amazed my sight.
I think, but dare not speak.

Gentlewoman. Good night, good doctor.

Exeunt

Andre. Ez nuke nai orrelako biotz bat bularrean euki gorputzak beregana lezaken nausitasun guziaren ordain ere.

Osagille. Ongi, ongi, ongi—

Andre. Eska ezaiozu Jainkoari orrela izan dedilla, jauna.

Osagille. Eritasun au nire jakintzaz gaiñekoa da. Ta, ala ere, lotan zebiltzala ta aien oetan santuki il ziran lagunak ezautu ditut.

MACBETH ANDREA. Garbi itzazu eskuok: jantzi gau-soiñekoa; ez
egon erren zurbillik. Berriz ere, esaten dizut, Banquo lurpetua dago, ezin irten diteke bere illobitik.

Osagille. Ba diteke ori?

MACBETH ANDREA. Oera, oera! Atea jotzen dute.
Zatoz, zatoz, zatoz, zatez. Ekazu eskua. Egiña ezin
liteke ezereztu. Oera, oera, oera.

Irtetzen da

Osagille. Oera joango al da?

Andre. Artez-artez.

Osagille. Zurrumurru nardagarriak dabiltz. Izaera-aurkako egintzaek izaera-kaltezko naspillak sortzen ditute. Gogo kutsatuek beren ixillekoak burko gorrai ematen dizkie. Bearrago du apaiza sendagille baiño. Jainkoa, Jainkoa, barka gaitzazu gu guzuiok! Zain ezazu. Ken ezaiozu bere buruari kalte egin dezaioken edozer eta izan ezazu beti begitan. Gabon, ba. Nire gogamenak begiak nastu ta izutu dizkit. Gogoetan ari naiz baiña ez dut itz egiteko kemenik.

Andre. Gabon osagille on.

Irtetzen dira

Scene 2

The country near Dunsinane.

Drum and colours. Enter MENTEITH, CAITHNESS, ANGUS, LENNOX, and Soldiers

MENTEITH. The English power is near, led on by Malcolm,
His uncle Siward and the good Macduff:
Revenges burn in them; for their dear causes
Would to the bleeding and the grim alarm
Excite the mortified man.

ANGUS. Near Birnam wood
Shall we well meet them; that way are they coming.

CAITHNESS. Who knows if Donalbain be with his brother?

LENNOX. For certain, sir, he is not: I have a file
Of all the gentry: there is Siward's son,
And many unrough youths that even now
Protest their first of manhood.

MENTEITH. What does the tyrant?

CAITHNESS. Great Dunsinane he strongly fortifies:
Some say he's mad; others that lesser hate him
Do call it valiant fury: but, for certain,
He cannot buckle his distemper'd cause
Within the belt of rule.

ANGUS. Now does he feel
His secret murders sticking on his hands;
Now minutely revolts upbraid his faith-breach;
Those he commands move only in command,
Nothing in love: now does he feel his title
Hang loose about him, like a giant's robe
Upon a dwarfish thief.

MENTEITH. Who then shall blame
His pester'd senses to recoil and start,

2'garren agerraldia

Dusinane'tik urbilleko zelaia.

MENTEITH, CAITHNESS, ANGUS, LENNOX eta gudariak sartzen dira, arratz eta ikurriñekin

MENTEITH. Gudarozte ingelandarra ba-dator,
Malcolm, onen osaba Siward eta Macduff bioztuna
buru dutela. Asper-miñak erretzen ditu. Izan ere, aien
biotzen bultzagaiek laster eragingo liokeke il bateri
gudatoki odoldu, ikaragarrira.

ANGUS. Birnam'eko basotik urbillean
arkituko ditugu, ortik datoz eta.

CAITHNESS. Iñork al daki Donalbain bere anaiarekin ote dagen?

LENNOX. Ez baldin ere, jauna. Ba-daukat
aundiki guzien errolda; aien artean Siward'en
semea ta gazte bizar gabe asko dira beren
gizontasuna aldarrikatzeko gertu daudenak.

MENTEITH. Tiranua zertan ari da?

CAITHNESS. Dunsinane'ko gaztelu aundia gogorki
sendotzen. Batzuek zoro dagola diote. Beste batzuek.
ura gutxiago gorrotatzen dutenek, guda-sumiñaz
mintzatzen dira. Baiña ziur ere, ezin dezake gerrikatu
bere auzi ertuna zuzenbidearen itoltzaz.

ANGUS. Ba-dakus orain bere ixilleko sarraskiek
eskuak lotzen dizkietela; miñutu bakoitzean gertatzen
diran matxinadek gaitzustea aurpegira ematen diotela.
Bere agindupekoak aginduaren eragitez bakarrik
ari diralako, ez maitasunez. Ba-dakus orain bere
erregetza inguruan zintzillik daukala, erraldoi
baten jantzia epo baten bizkarrean bezela.

MENTEITH. Nork gaitzetsiko ditu, beraz,
aren zentzun mindunak gibelka ta

When all that is within him does condemn
Itself for being there?

CAITHNESS. Well, march we on,
To give obedience where 'tis truly owed:
Meet we the medicine of the sickly weal,
And with him pour we in our country's purge
Each drop of us.

LENNOX. Or so much as it needs,
To dew the sovereign flower and drown the weeds.
Make we our march towards Birnam.

Exeunt, marching

Act 5, Scene 3

Dunsinane. A room in the castle. Enter MACBETH, doctor, and attendants

MACBETH. Bring me no more reports; let them fly all:
Till Birnam wood remove to Dunsinane,
I cannot taint with fear. What's the boy Malcolm?
Was he not born of woman? The spirits that know
All mortal consequences have pronounced me thus:
"Fear not, Macbeth; no man that's born of woman
Shall e'er have power upon thee." Then fly, false thanes,
And mingle with the English epicures:
The mind I sway by and the heart I bear
Shall never sag with doubt nor shake with fear.

Enter a Servant

The devil damn thee black, thou cream-faced loon!
Where got'st thou that goose look?

Servant. here is ten thousand—

MACBETH. Geese, villain!

Servant. Soldiers, sir.

iraulka ari diralako, beregan dan guziak antxe itxia egotearen lotsa artzez ba'du?

CAITHNESS. Goazen aurrera, ba, gure menpetasuna ematera zor zaionari. Goazen jaurerri gaiso onen osagilleagana ta isuriko ditugu arekin gure odol tanta guziak aberria osatzeko.

LENNOX. Beiñik-bein, erregetzaren lorea zirtatu ta galbelarra itotzeko bear dan aiña. Goazen Birnam'erantz!

Irtetzen dira gudari eraz

5'garren atala. 3'garren agerraldia

Dunsinane. Gazteluko gela bat. MACBETH, osagillea ta otseiñak sartzen dira

MACBETH. Ez ekarri niri berri geiago. Igesi dioazela guziak! Birnam'eko basoa Dusinane'ra etorri ez dedin arte, ez nau beldurrak kutsatuko. Nor da Malcolm mutil ori? Ez al du emakumegandik jaio? Giza-izango guziak ezagunak dituten izpirituak onela mintzatu ziran: "Ez beldur izan, Macbeth, emakumegandik jaioriko gizonek ez dizu iñoiz gaiña artuko." Itzuri, beraz, thane etoi oriek, eta nastu zaitezte ingelandar epikurutarrekin. Ez bidatzen nau gogoak, ezta daramadan biotz au ere ez dira ezmezaz okilduko ez beldurrez ikaratuko.

Otsein bat sartzen da

Txerrenak beltzituko al au! Esnegain-aurpegiko doillor ori! Nondik dakark antzar aurpegi ori?

Otsein. Ba-dira amar milla—

MACBETH. Ate, ergel ori!

Otsein. Gudari, jauna.

MACBETH. Go prick thy face, and over-red thy fear,
Thou lily-liver'd boy. What soldiers, patch?
Death of thy soul! those linen cheeks of thine
Are counsellors to fear. What soldiers, whey-face?

Servant. The English force, so please you.

MACBETH. Take thy face hence.

Exit Servant

Seyton!—I am sick at heart,
When I behold—Seyton, I say!—This push
Will cheer me ever, or disseat me now.
I have lived long enough: my way of life
Is fall'n into the sear, the yellow leaf;
And that which should accompany old age,
As honour, love, obedience, troops of friends,
I must not look to have; but, in their stead,
Curses, not loud but deep, mouth-honour, breath,
Which the poor heart would fain deny, and dare not. Seyton!

Enter SEYTON

SEYTON. What is your gracious pleasure?

MACBETH. What news more?

SEYTON. All is confirm'd, my lord, which was reported.

MACBETH. I'll fight till from my bones my flesh be hack'd.
Give me my armour.

SEYTON. 'Tis not needed yet.

MACBETH. I'll put it on.
Send out more horses; skirr the country round;
Hang those that talk of fear. Give me mine armour.
How does your patient, doctor?

MACBETH. Oa, estal ezak aurpegia ta margotu gorriz ire beldurra, umekondo gibelegille ori! Nolako gudariak, alotza? Birao iri! Ire masail zurbilla latz-ikararen aolkariak dituk. Nolako gudariak, esnezko aurpegi ori?

Otsein. Ingelanda'ko gudari saillak, gaitzi ez ba'zaizu.

MACBETH. Alde nire aurretik

Otseiña joaten da

Seyton!—Biotza jauzi egiten dit dakusdanean—
Seyton, esan dut—Eraso onek betiko goraipatuko
nau ala jauralkitik jaurtiko! Naikoa bizi izan naiz;
nire bizitzaren bidea osto orixkako
udazkenarantz etziten da, ta zartzaroa inguratu
bearko luken guzi ori; begirunea, maitasuna,
mentasuna, adiskideen jarraigoa ez dut itxaro
bear; bai, ordea, birao itoak baiña barnak,
zurikerizko itzak, biotz gaisoak astandu nai ta
ikutu ezin ditzaken murmurak. Seyton!

SEYTON sartzen da

SEYTON. Zer atsegin, errege jauna?

MACBETH. Zer berri geiago?

SEYTON. Artu ditugun berri guziak egizta'tu dira.

MACBETH. Burrukatuko naiz aragia nire ezurretatik askatu dedin arte. Emaidazu guda-jantzia.

SEYTON. Ez duzu oraiño aren bearrik.

MACBETH. Jantziko dut.
Bidaldu zaldizko geiago inguruak ikuskatzera.
Urka ditzatela beldurrez mintzatzen diranak. Emaidazu guda-jantzia! Hola doa zure geisoa, osagille ori?

Doctor. Not so sick, my lord,
As she is troubled with thick coming fancies,
That keep her from her rest.

MACBETH. Cure her of that.
Canst thou not minister to a mind diseased,
Pluck from the memory a rooted sorrow,
Raze out the written troubles of the brain
And with some sweet oblivious antidote
Cleanse the stuff'd bosom of that perilous stuff
Which weighs upon the heart?

Doctor. Therein the patient
Must minister to himself.

MACBETH. Throw physic to the dogs; I'll none of it.
Come, put mine armour on; give me my staff.
Seyton, send out. Doctor, the thanes fly from me.
Come, sir, dispatch. If thou couldst, doctor, cast
The water of my land, find her disease,
And purge it to a sound and pristine health,
I would applaud thee to the very echo,
That should applaud again.—Pull't off, I say.—
What rhubarb, cyme, or what purgative drug,
Would scour these English hence? Hear'st thou of them?

Doctor. Ay, my good lord; your royal preparation
Makes us hear something.

MACBETH. Bring it after me.
I will not be afraid of death and bane,
Till Birnam forest come to Dunsinane.

Doctor. [Aside] Were I from Dunsinane away and clear,
Profit again should hardly draw me here.

Exeunt

Osagille. Bere gaitza ez da ain aundia, jauna;
baiña sarritan nastutzen duten irudikeriek
atsedena galerazten diote.

MACBETH. Osatu ezazu. Ez al dezakezu
gago ertun bat gozatu, bere oroimenetik
arroztatutako naigabeak idoki, burumuiñean
idatzi ziñak eta miñak ezabatu, ta sendagaillu
ezti, aztu-erazle batekin bere biotzaren
gaiñean astuntzen diran zama kaltegiñetik
bularra garbitu?

Osagille. Orrelakoetan geisoak
bere buruaren osagille izan bear du.

MACBETH. Jaurtazu sendakintza txakurrei! ez dut aren bearrik! Zatoz, ipiñi ezaidazu burdin-jantzia. Emaidazu nire agintza-makilla. Seyton atera ditezela. Osagille, thaneak uzten naute. Ots, jauna, laster egin! Osagille, nire erreiñuaren gernua azterkatu, aren eritasuna arkitu ta erin gaiaren bidez lenagoko osasun bikaiña ari atzera eman al ba'zenezaio txalo egingo nizuke, oiartzun guziek nire txaloak berregin arte!... Kentzeko esan dizut! Nongo arabarbak pitugarrik naiz droga eringarrik garbitu dezake ingelandarrez erri au? Ezautzen al duzu bat-edo-bat?

Osagille. Bai, jaun ori; zure erregeren gertakuntzak
entzun erazten digu zerbait.

MACBETH. Ken ori nire aurretik.
Ez diot eriotzari ez elkaitzari beldur izan bear
Birnam'eko oiana Dusinane'ra datorren arte.

Osagille. [Berezian] Dusinane'tik naierara irten al ba'nendi,
ez nintzake onara itzuliko ez urre ez zillar orde.

Irtetzen da

Scene 4

Country near Birnam wood.

Drum and colours. Enter MALCOLM, SIWARD and YOUNG SIWARD, MACDUFF, MENTEITH, CAITHNESS, ANGUS, LENNOX, ROSS, and Soldiers, marching

MALCOLM. Cousins, I hope the days are near at hand
That chambers will be safe.

MENTEITH. We doubt it nothing.

SIWARD. What wood is this before us?

MENTEITH. The wood of Birnam.

MALCOLM. Let every soldier hew him down a bough
And bear't before him: thereby shall we shadow
The numbers of our host and make discovery
Err in report of us.

Soldiers. It shall be done.

SIWARD. We learn no other but the confident tyrant
Keeps still in Dunsinane, and will endure
Our setting down before 't.

MALCOLM. 'Tis his main hope:
For where there is advantage to be given,
Both more and less have given him the revolt,
And none serve with him but constrained things
Whose hearts are absent too.

MACDUFF. Let our just censures
Attend the true event, and put we on
Industrious soldiership.

SIWARD. The time approaches
That will with due decision make us know

4'garren agerraldia

Zelai bat Birnam'eko oian aldean.

MALCOLM, SIWARD zarra ta bere semea, MACDUFF, MENTEITH, CAITHNESS, ANGUS, LENNOX, ROSS eta Gudariak sartzen dira arratz eta ikurriñekin

MALCOLM. Aideok, gure gelak leku ziurrak izango ditugun eguna urbil dugu, nik uste.

MENTEITH. Ez dugu dudarik.

SIWARD. Zein oian da gure aurreko au?

MENTEITH. Birnam'eko oiana.

MALCOLM. Gudari bakoitzak adar bat ebaki
ta bere aurrean eraman dezala, onela gure
gudareztearen kopurua estali ta etsaien
zelatariei uts eragingo diegu.

GUDARIAK. Orixe egingo dugu.

SIWARD. Dekigunetik, tiranua ustantzaz betea,
Dusinane'n dugu beti ta gogor egingo dio gure
moltzoari.

MALCOLM. Ori da aren itxaropide
aundiena; mugona duteneko aundiak
eta txikiak jauzten zazkio. Ertsatuak
baizik ez dira aren morrointzan ari ta
auen biotzak urruti daude argandik.

MACDUFF. Utzi ditzagun bidezko
espenak gertaria etorri dediñeko ta
erabilli dezagun gudari-jakintza.

SIWARD. Zor-artzekoak argi ezautuko
ditugun ordua ba-datorkigu. Irudimenak

What we shall say we have and what we owe.
Thoughts speculative their unsure hopes relate,
But certain issue strokes must arbitrate:
Towards which advance the war.

Exeunt, marching

Scene 5

Dunsinane. Within the castle.

Enter MACBETH, SEYTON, and Soldiers, with drum and colours

MACBETH. Hang out our banners on the outward walls;
The cry is still "They come:" our castle's strength
Will laugh a siege to scorn: here let them lie
Till famine and the ague eat them up:
Were they not forced with those that should be ours,
We might have met them dareful, beard to beard,
And beat them backward home.

A cry of women within

What is that noise?

SEYTON. It is the cry of women, my good lord.

Exit SEYTON

MACBETH. I have almost forgot the taste of fears;
The time has been, my senses would have cool'd
To hear a night-shriek; and my fell of hair
Would at a dismal treatise rouse and stir
As life were in't: I have supp'd full with horrors;
Direness, familiar to my slaughterous thoughts
Cannot once start me.

Re-enter SEYTON

Wherefore was that cry?

SEYTON. The queen, my lord, is dead.

ezbaiko itxaropenez poztutzen gaitu,
baiña ukaldiek egizko ondorea
erabakitzen dute.
Guda muga ortara doa.

Irtetzen dira gudari-ibilkeraz

5'garren agerraldia

Dunsinane'n. Gaztelu barruan.

MACBETH, SEYTON eta Gudariak sartzen dira arratz eta ikurriñarekin.

MACBETH. Zabaldu gure ikurriñak lekoreko arresien gaiñean. Didarra "Badatoz!" da beti, baiña gure gazteluaren indarrak irri egingo dio erdeiñuz aien moltsoari. Daudela or, sukarrak eta goseak irentsi ditzaten arte! Gureak izan bearko lirakenakin lagunduta ez ba'leude, aien billa joango giñan ausarki, aurpegiz-aurpegi ta aien etxeetaraiño esti eragin genezaieke.

Emakumezko ouiak barruan

Zer zarata da ori?

SEYTON. Emakumezko ouiak dira, jaun ori.

SEYTON Irtetzen da

MACBETH. Beldurraren aogozoaz aztuxe naiz.
Aldi batean nire zentzunak izoztutzen ziran gau-
karraisi bat entzuteaz eta nire buruko illeak
zutitu ta laztu egiten ziran, bizidunak bai'liran,
ipuin ikaragarri batekin. Asebete naiz lazturaz!
Ikaragarria etxeko dut nire eriozko gogapenetan
eta ezin dezaidake zirrararik eman.

SEYTON sartzen da berriz

Zer dala ta oiuok?

SEYTON. Jauna, erregiña il da.

MACBETH. She should have died hereafter;
There would have been a time for such a word.
To-morrow, and to-morrow, and to-morrow,
Creeps in this petty pace from day to day
To the last syllable of recorded time,
And all our yesterdays have lighted fools
The way to dusty death. Out, out, brief candle!
Life's but a walking shadow, a poor player
That struts and frets his hour upon the stage
And then is heard no more: it is a tale
Told by an idiot, full of sound and fury,
Signifying nothing.

Enter a Messenger

Thou comest to use thy tongue; thy story quickly.

Messenger. Gracious my lord,
I should report that which I say I saw,
But know not how to do it.

MACBETH. Well, say, sir.

Messenger. As I did stand my watch upon the hill,
I look'd toward Birnam, and anon, methought,
The wood began to move.

MACBETH. Liar and slave!

Messenger. Let me endure your wrath, if't be not so:
Within this three mile may you see it coming;
I say, a moving grove.

MACBETH. If thou speak'st false,
Upon the next tree shalt thou hang alive,
Till famine cling thee: if thy speech be sooth,
I care not if thou dost for me as much.
I pull in resolution, and begin
To doubt the equivocation of the fiend
That lies like truth: "Fear not, till Birnam wood
Do come to Dunsinane:" and now a wood

MACBETH. Geroxeago il bear zukean. Ordun
aldia izango nuan orrelako itza aditzeko. Biar
ta biar ta biar ba-doaz aurrera urrats xean
egunetik egunera, oroitu diteken aldiaren
azken itzaren zatiraiño, ta gure atzo guziek
eriotz-autserako bidea argi egin diote zoroei.
Itzungi zaitez, itzungi zuzi igeskor ori! Bizitza
igaroten dan itzala besterik ez da, agertokian
ordu betean zaloika ta igika ari dan
antzezlari gaiso bat eta gero entzuten ez dana;
ergel batek kontatutako ipuiña, soiñuz eta
sumiñez ta ezer esan nai ez duna.

Gudari bat sartzen da

Mingaiña erabiltzeko ator, ire ixtoria, ba, arin!

Gudari. Nire jaun ona,
esan nai nizuke esango dizudana ikusi dudala,
baiña ez dakit nola.

MACBETH. Ongi, esan, jauna.

Gudari. Muruan begirari nengoalarik,
Birnam aldea so egin dut eta berberean
oiana igitzen asten zala iduri zait.

MACBETH. Gezurrontzi ta doillorra!

Gudari. Jasan dezadala zure aserrea baldin orrela ez ba'da.
Emendik iru legoa ikusi dezakezu etortzen.
Bai, egitan, oian bat ba-dabil.

MACBETH. Gezur ba'diok urbilleneko zugatzetik
zintzilika jarriko aut bizirik gosez igartu adin arte.
Diokana egia ba'da, egin dezakek beste orren-beste
nirekin, ezer ez zaidak. Nire adorea kordokatzen da
ta egiaren zomorro pean gezur dion deabruaren
iruzurra usmatzen asten naiz. "Ez beldurrik izan
Birman'eko oiana Dusinane'ra etorri dedin arte." Ta
orain oian bat Dusinane'rantz dator. Izkilluak artu!,

Comes toward Dunsinane. Arm, arm, and out!
If this which he avouches does appear,
There is nor flying hence nor tarrying here.
I gin to be aweary of the sun,
And wish the estate o' the world were now undone.
Ring the alarum-bell! Blow, wind! come, wrack!
At least we'll die with harness on our back.

Exeunt

Scene 6

Dunsinane. Before the castle.

Drum and colours. Enter MALCOLM, SIWARD, MACDUFF, and their Army, with boughs

MALCOLM. Now near enough: your leafy screens throw down.
And show like those you are. You, worthy uncle,
Shall, with my cousin, your right-noble son,
Lead our first battle: worthy Macduff and we
Shall take upon 's what else remains to do,
According to our order.

SIWARD. Fare you well.
Do we but find the tyrant's power to-night,
Let us be beaten, if we cannot fight.

MACDUFF. Make all our trumpets speak; give them all breath,
Those clamorous harbingers of blood and death.

Exeunt

Act 5, Scene 7

Another part of the field. Alarums. Enter MACBETH

MACBETH. They have tied me to a stake; I cannot fly,
But, bear-like, I must fight the course. What's he
That was not born of woman? Such a one
Am I to fear, or none.

Izkilluak artu! Baldin egia ba'da onek diona berdin zait . . . emendik iges egitea ala gelditzea. Eguzkia ikusteaz aspertzen asi naiz dagoneko, ta munduaren goiberatu dedilla irrikitzen nago. Jozute guda ezkilla!
Putz egin aize orrek!
Ator ondamena! Altziru-jantzia soiñean dugula
igo gera, beiñik bein!

Irtetzen dira

6'garren agerraldia

Dusinane. Gaztelu aurrean.

MALCOLM, SIWARD zarra, MACDUFF eta beren gudaroztea sartzen dira zugatz-adar ata arratz eta ikurriñekin

MALCOLM. Ba-gera urbil. Jaurti itzazute zuen ostozko itzalkiek eta ager zaitezte zeratenez. Zu, osaba jator orrek, nire lengusu, zure seme oso zintzoarekin, gure lenengo gudari taldea aginduko duzu. Macduff bioztunak eta nik gaiñerakoa gure gain artuko dugu, gure asmoaren arauz.

SIWARD. Agur!
Arkituko al ditugu arratsalde ontan tiranuaren gudariak
eta ondatu nadilla baldin burrukatzen ez ba'dakigu!

MACDUFF. Gure turuta guziek ots dagitela! Emaiezute zuen arnas guzia odol eta eriotzaren berri eramaille deadartsu oriei!

Irtetzen dira

5'garren atala. 7'garren agerraldia

Gudatekiko beste leku bat. MACBETH sartzen da.

MACBETH. Abe batean lotu naute; iges egiterik ez daukat, baiña artza iduri oldarrari gogor egin bear diot. Nun dago emakumegandik ez jaioa? Orretxen beldur izan bear dut eta ez beste iñoren.

Enter YOUNG SIWARD

YOUNG SIWARD. What is thy name?

MACBETH. Thou'lt be afraid to hear it.

YOUNG SIWARD. No; though thou call'st thyself a hotter name
Than any is in hell.

MACBETH. My name's Macbeth.

YOUNG SIWARD. The devil himself could not pronounce a title
More hateful to mine ear.

MACBETH. No, nor more fearful.

YOUNG SIWARD. Thou liest, abhorred tyrant; with my sword
I'll prove the lie thou speak'st.

They fight and YOUNG SIWARD is slain

MACBETH. Thou wast born of woman
But swords I smile at, weapons laugh to scorn,
Brandish'd by man that's of a woman born.

Exit

Alarums. Enter MACDUFF

MACDUFF. That way the noise is. Tyrant, show thy face!
If thou be'st slain and with no stroke of mine,
My wife and children's ghosts will haunt me still.
I cannot strike at wretched kerns, whose arms
Are hired to bear their staves: either thou, Macbeth,
Or else my sword with an unbatter'd edge
I sheathe again undeeded. There thou shouldst be;
By this great clatter, one of greatest note
Seems bruited. Let me find him, fortune!
And more I beg not.

SIWARD GAZTEA sartzen da

SIWARD GAZTEA. Xela duk izena?

MACBETH. Ikaratuke intzake ura entzuteaz!

SIWARD GAZTEA. Ez, inpernuko edozeiñena baiño gartsuaso bat ba'u ere.

MACBETH. Macbeth diat izena.

SIWARD GAZTEA. Txerrenak berak ez likek nire belarriendako izen gorrotagarriagorik esango.

MACBETH. Ez ezta beldurgarriagorik ere.

SIWARD GAZTEA. Gezur diek, tiranu madarikatu ori, nire ezpataz egiztatuko diat ire gezurra.

Burrukatzen ari dira ta SIWARD GAZTEA iltzen da

MACBETH. Emakumegandik jaioa intzan.
Emakumegandik jaiotako edozein gizonen ezpataeri ta
izkilluei irri ta muzin egiten diet!

Irtetzen da

MACDUFF sartzen da

MACDUFF. Emendik dator dunbotsa. Tiranu
ori, erakutsi ire aurpegia. Nire eskuz iltzen ez
ba'aiz, nire emazte ta aurren itzalak estu
eraziko natxiotek beti. Ez dizkiat jo nai,
makilla eramateko besoa alogeratu dizkitekan
lagun errukarriak. I, Macbeth, ala ezpata
zorroratuko diat garbi ta alperra, ortik edo
abil, deadarka orrek lagun nabariren bat
iragarri bide du. Ekardazu ona, Zoria,
ta ez dizut geiago eskatzen.

Exit. Alarums

Enter MALCOLM and SIWARD

SIWARD. This way, my lord; the castle's gently render'd:
The tyrant's people on both sides do fight;
The noble thanes do bravely in the war;
The day almost itself professes yours,
And little is to do.

MALCOLM. We have met with foes
That strike beside us.

SIWARD. Enter, sir, the castle.

Exeunt. Alarums

Act 5, Scene 8

Another part of the field. Enter MACBETH

MACBETH. Why should I play the Roman fool, and die
On mine own sword? whiles I see lives, the gashes
Do better upon them.

Enter MACDUFF

MACDUFF. Turn, hell-hound, turn!

MACBETH. Of all men else I have avoided thee:
But get thee back; my soul is too much charged
With blood of thine already.

MACDUFF. I have no words:
My voice is in my sword: thou bloodier villain
Than terms can give thee out!

They fight

MACBETH. Thou losest labour:
As easy mayst thou the intrenchant air
With thy keen sword impress as make me bleed:

Irtetzen da. Turutotsak

MALCOLM eta SIWARD zarra sartzen dira

SIWARD. Emendik, jauna! Gazteluak txil egin du burruka gabe. Tiranuaren gudariak gudarozte bietan ari dira burrukatzen. Thane zintzoek beren eginbearra betetzen dute azkarki. Egunak berak zure alde agertzeko urrean dago ta egitekorik gutxi dugu.

MALCOLM. Arkitu ditugun etsaiak gure
alde burrukatzen ari dira.

SIWARD. Sar gaitezen gaztelura, jauna.

Irtetzen dira. Turutotsak

5'garren atala. 8'garren agerraldia

Gudatekiko beste leku bat. MACBETH sartzen da berriz.

MACBETH. Zertako egingo nuke eroarena, Erromatar bat antzo ta neronen ezpata pean il? Bizidunak ikusten ditudan artean aiztokadak enetzat baiño aientzat obe.

MACDUFF sartzen da

MACDUFF. Itzul adi, inpernu-txakur ori, itzul!

MACBETH. Guzien artean orandik alde egin diat bakarrik.
Oa! Gogoa zamatuegi zeukat
iretarren odolez.

MACDUFF. Ez diat itzik.
Ezpatan diat itza, i, mingaiñak esan zezaken
gaizkin odolkoien ori!

Borrokatzen dira

MACBETH. Alperriko lana!
Errezago izango atzait aize zauritu eziña ire ezpata
zorrotzaz xakitzea niri odola ateraztea baiño. Utzak

Let fall thy blade on vulnerable crests;
I bear a charmed life, which must not yield,
To one of woman born.

MACDUFF. Despair thy charm;
And let the angel whom thou still hast served
Tell thee, Macduff was from his mother's womb
Untimely ripp'd.

MACBETH. Accursed be that tongue that tells me so,
For it hath cow'd my better part of man!
And be these juggling fiends no more believed,
That palter with us in a double sense;
That keep the word of promise to our ear,
And break it to our hope. I'll not fight with thee.

MACDUFF. Then yield thee, coward,
And live to be the show and gaze o' the time:
We'll have thee, as our rarer monsters are,
Painted on a pole, and underwrit,
"Here may you see the tyrant."

MACBETH. I will not yield,
To kiss the ground before young Malcolm's feet,
And to be baited with the rabble's curse.
Though Birnam wood be come to Dunsinane,
And thou opposed, being of no woman born,
Yet I will try the last. Before my body
I throw my warlike shield. Lay on, Macduff,
And damn'd be him that first cries, "Hold, enough!"

Exeunt, fighting. Alarums. Retreat.
Flourish.
Enter, with drum and colours, MALCOLM, SIWARD, ROSS, the other Thanes, and Soldiers

MALCOLM. I would the friends we miss were safe arrived.

SIWARD. Some must go off: and yet, by these I see,
So great a day as this is cheaply bought.

ire altzairua erortzen buru zaurigarrien gaiñera. Bizia sorgindua diat eta emakumegandik jaiotako gizon bateri ezin txil egin.

MACDUFF. Ez entzindu sorginkeri ortatik, eta beti morroi egin diokan gaitzaren aingeruak esan bezaik Macduff garaiz aurretik idokia izan uala bere amaren sabeletik.

MACBETH. Madarikatua ori ageri egin didan mingaiña! Nire gizon zati obea oillotu erazi du. Ta ez al die egun eta eguzki ziñetsiko zimardikaz ziria sartzen diguten deabru iruzurgilleok, itza atxikitzen dutenak gure belarriendako ta jaten gure itxarobiderako. Ez nauk irekin burrukatuko.

MACDUFF. Txil egik, ba, koldar orrek. Eta bizi adi gizonen begiragarri ta parregarri izateko. Ire-margo irudia ipiñiko diagu aga baten gaiñean, mamu bakan baten antzera ta "Emen ikusi dezakezute tiranua" idatziko azpian.

MACBETH. Ez diat txil egingo, Malcolm gazteak oinpetu lurrari musu emateko ta lagunabarren biraooz aizatua izateko. Nai ta Birnam'eko Dusinane'ra etorri ta i emakumegandik jaioa ez izan, azkeneko alegiña egingo diat. Nire gorputzaren aurrean guda babesa jartzen dut. Jo, ba, Macduff, ta madarikatua izan bedi aurrenik "Gel, aski!" ots egin dezana.

Irtetzen dira burrukan. Turutotsa.
MALCOLM, SIWARD zarra, ROSS, LENNOX, ANGUS, CAITHNESS, MENTEITH eta gudariak sartzen dira berriz arratz eta ikurriñekin.

MALCOLM. Nai nuke emen ez diran adiskideak oro ta sendo egotea.

SIWARD. Bai ta ezkoa da zenbait iltzea, ta ala ere, emen diranak ikusi ta merke erosi dugu agun aundi au.

MALCOLM. Macduff is missing, and your noble son.

ROSS. Your son, my lord, has paid a soldier's debt:
He only lived but till he was a man;
The which no sooner had his prowess confirm'd
In the unshrinking station where he fought,
But like a man he died.

SIWARD. Then he is dead?

ROSS. Ay, and brought off the field: your cause of sorrow
Must not be measured by his worth, for then
It hath no end.

SIWARD. Had he his hurts before?

ROSS. Ay, on the front.

SIWARD. Why then, God's soldier be he!
Had I as many sons as I have hairs,
I would not wish them to a fairer death:
And so, his knell is knoll'd.

MALCOLM. He's worth more sorrow,
And that I'll spend for him.

SIWARD. He's worth no more
They say he parted well, and paid his score:
And so, God be with him! Here comes newer comfort.

Re-enter MACDUFF, with MACBETH's head

MACDUFF. Hail, king! for so thou art: behold, where stands
The usurper's cursed head: the time is free:
I see thee compass'd with thy kingdom's pearl,
That speak my salutation in their minds;
Whose voices I desire aloud with mine:
Hail, King of Scotland!

ALL. Hail, King of Scotland!

MALCOLM. Macduff eta zure seme zintzoak ez dira.

ROSS. Zure semeak, jauna, bere gudari zorra ordaindu du. Ez da bizi izan gizon izan zan arte baizik. Bere kemenaz ba-zala egietan eman zunekoxe atzeka egin gabe burrukatu zan lekuan erori zan gizon gisa.

SIWARD. Il da, beraz?

ROSS. Bai, ta gudatokitik aldendu dute.
Zure miña ezin nuertu dezakezu aren mereziaz,
ez lukelako ordun amairik.

SIWARD. Aurretik sakaildu al zuten?

ROSS. Bai, aurpegiz aurpegi.

SIWARD. Ortara ezkero, Jainkoaren gudari izan bedi!
Illerik aiña seme ba'nitu, ez nieke
eriotz ederragorik opa izango.
Ta onekin aren il ezkillak jo du.

MALCOLM. Deitore geiago merezi
du ta nigandik eukiko.

SIWARD. Ez du geiagorik merezi.
Ongi joana omen da ta bere zerga ordaindu du.
Emen datorkigu pozbide berri bat.

MACDUFF sartzen da MACBETH'en burua dakarrela

MACDUFF. Agur, errege, ba-zera ta! Ara nun duzun sasi-nagusiaren buru madarikatua. Gizartea bere eskuko da. Ba-zakust jauregiko pitxiz inguratua nire agurra beren gogoetan esaten dutenak. Beren mintzoak, nirearekin batean ots dagitela gogorki; Agur, Eskotelande'ko errege ori.

GUZIAK. Agur, Eskotelande'ko errege ori!

Flourish

MALCOLM. We shall not spend a large expense of time
Before we reckon with your several loves,
And make us even with you. My thanes and kinsmen,
Henceforth be earls, the first that ever Scotland
In such an honour named. What's more to do,
Which would be planted newly with the time,
As calling home our exiled friends abroad
That fled the snares of watchful tyranny;
Producing forth the cruel ministers
Of this dead butcher and his fiend-like queen,
Who, as 'tis thought, by self and violent hands
Took off her life; this, and what needful else
That calls upon us, by the grace of Grace,
We will perform in measure, time and place:
So, thanks to all at once and to each one,
Whom we invite to see us crown'd at Scone.

Flourish. Exeunt

The End

Turuta otsa

MALCOLM. Ez duu aldi asko emango zuen oneriztearekin
artu-emanak garbitu ta zuei ordaiña
eman gabe. Ene thane ta aideek: gaurdanik kondeak
izango zerate, Eskotelanda'n deitura au
eramango duten lenbizikoak. Egiteko dagona ta
aldi berrien arauz bururatu bear dana, ots, tiranukeri
zelatari baten sareetatik iges egin zuten
gure adiskide esbestetuei dei egitea; arakin il
onen eta beraren esku gogorrez bere burua il zun
aren erregiña deabrudunaren esku-ordeko ankerrak
argitara ekartzea, au ta guri dagokigun
eta egin bearra dan guzia, Jainkoa'ren eskerraz,
bere neurrian, aldian eta lekuan egingo dugu.
Gure eskerrona guziei ta bakoitzari, ta dei egiten
dizuet Scone'n gure koroatzea ikustera etorri
zaitezten.

Turuta-otsak. Irtetzen dira

Amaiera

www.ingramcontent.com/pod-product-compliance
Lightning Source LLC
LaVergne TN
LVHW010056110826
845155LV00028B/370

* 9 7 8 1 9 3 5 7 0 9 7 2 5 *